THE
SHARIYAT
-KI-
SUGMAD
Book One

Authorized ECKANKAR edition.

THE
SHARIYAT
-KI-
SUGMAD

Book One

Paul Twitchell

Illuminated Way
Publishing Inc.
PO Box 28130
Crystal, MN 55428

THE SHARIYAT-KI-SUGMAD
Book One

Copyright © 1970, 1987 ECKANKAR

Printed in U.S.A.
ISBN: 0-88155-053-1

Second Edition—1987

Tenth Printing—1987

Dedicated to

The ECK Masters of
the Ancient Order of Vairagi,
who waited patiently for the right
time to give this message to the world.

THE SHARIYAT-KI-SUGMAD, Book One

THE ANCIENT SCRIPTURES OF ECKANKAR, the Science of Soul Travel brought to light for the first time.

These writings of golden wisdom which have always been hidden in the spiritual worlds have now been translated and published for the first time.

Book One is the first section of the works of the SHARIYAT-KI-SUGMAD which was dictated by Sri Fubbi Quantz, the great ECK Master, who serves at the Katsupari Monastery in northern Tibet. Twelve or more volumes of the SHARIYAT-KI-SUGMAD will be published.

The SHARIYAT-KI-SUGMAD contains the wisdom and ecstatic knowledge of those planes of the spiritual worlds, beyond the regions of time and space. To read and study this highly inspired book will give the reader an insight into the scriptures found in the Temples of Golden Wisdom.

The essence of God-knowledge is laid down in these writings. Those who follow ECK are involved in the SHARIYAT-KI-SUGMAD for it is their bible, their everlasting gospel. All worldly doctrines on religions, philosophies, and sacred writings are offspring of the SHARIYAT-KI-SUGMAD.

Contents

Introduction

The SHARIYAT-KI-SUGMAD, which means the "Way of the Eternal," is the ancient scripture of ECKANKAR, the science of Soul Travel and total consciousness.

It is possibly the oldest scripture known on earth. The Sanskrit writings, such as the Vedas, Upanishads, and Mahabharata, cannot be traced beyond four thousand years on this planet.

The SHARIYAT-KI-SUGMAD is said to have been known in antediluvian times, and before that on the so-called mythical continents known to us as Lemuria and Atlantis.

The Naacal records are reported to be among the first religious writings known to us, and they contain scattered references to ECKANKAR, or total consciousness.

Only two monasteries, one in the remote mountains of Tibet, and the other along the eastern slopes of the Hindu Kush mountains, have any of these writings in their keeping on this physical planet. Other sections of the SHARIYAT are located on other planets and on other planes beyond this world.

These monasteries are so well hidden that it is doubtful anyone could find them, not even the Buddhist lamas who have the power to move about in the ethers at will. The keepers of these records are so careful in their guardianship that no one can enter these monasteries unless they are first screened by the monks, who can read the seeker's aura like we scan a daily newspaper.

Sections of the SHARIYAT-KI-SUGMAD, the guide for those who wish to reach the heavenly kingdom via the route of ECKANKAR, are kept in each Temple of Golden Wisdom, beginning on this Earth planet and continuing on each spiritual plane upward into the very heart of the Kingdom of God.

It is mainly kept—here on the Earth planet—in the spiritual city of Agam Des, which lies in the high wilderness of the Hindu Kush mountains in Central Asia. Only those who are able to travel in the Atma Sarup, the Soul body, can reach this extraordinary community of Adepts and study these ancient scriptures of truth.

ECKANKAR is the basic foundation for all religions, philosophies, and scientific works in our world today. It is closer to being in its original form, as the science of Soul Travel, than any of the other paths to God. However, it is not just religion, philosophy, or metaphysics, for it is the ECK Marg, meaning the path of ECKANKAR.

It has been handed down by word of mouth from Rama, the first known world savior, who came out of the deep forests of northern Germany and traveled down to Persia, where he paused long enough to give these secret teachings to a few mystics whose descendants were to become the followers of Zoroaster, the Persian sage.

Rama then proceeded to India, where he settled and taught that man could have the experience of God in his own lifetime.

ECKANKAR was revealed to Rama by one of the ancient ECK Masters. It is likely that he was lifted out of the body and taken to the city of Agam Des, where the SHARIYAT-KI-SUGMAD was shown him and he was given the opportunity to study its contents.

No written instructions were available to the followers

xii

of ECKANKAR until about the thirteenth century, when Jalal-ud-din'l-Rumi, the mystic poet of Persia, hinted at it in his great poem, "The Reed of God."

In about the sixteenth century, Kabir, the Hindu mystic poet, took it upon himself to unwrap the mysteries of the Ancient Science of Soul Travel.

He had quite a time with his adversaries, for everybody who believed in orthodox religion thought he was crazy and many tried to kill him. Those who were followers of the science of Soul Travel knew he was wrong to try to reveal such truth at that time. As a result, he was hounded until he could scarcely keep himself alive, spending most of his time in hiding.

There was a corruption of the original teachings by word of mouth, and several other paths came out of this. Some of these were Shabda Yoga, the Magi, the cult of Dionysus, and a few other mystery schools that are generally well known to us. Each school of divine knowledge branched off into its own particular way as a path to God. The six great religious systems of India are only branches of the God-Vidya (God-knowledge) that we call ECK. So are the religions of the West and every continent, including Africa and Asia. A study of *The Golden Bough,* by Frazer will bear this out.

Basically, the main principle, or vital part, of ECKANKAR is out-of-the-consciousness projection, which is far beyond the astral or any other lower-plane movements.

It has been corrupted from the original source as man developed it in various parts of the world into a semblance of religion and worship. Man thus fell away from the main stream of truth and created his own gods and rituals. Thus we find that there is some truth in the story about the Tower of Babel.

The SHARIYAT-KI-SUGMAD consists of about twelve

books, each book, on the inner planes, comprising twelve to fifteen chapters. These chapters average about thirty thousand words and are made up of cantos, or what we call verse in dialogue form, in which the SUGMAD (God) speaks to ITS chief disciple, Sat Nam, sometimes called the Sat Purusha, lord of the spiritual plane of Soul, or the fifth region. He is believed by some to be the supreme SUGMAD but is only the first manifestation of God.

Not all the writing is made up of cantos or free verse. Often it is in straight narrative, or legends and stories. Sometimes it is in allegories or fables. But altogether it is the whole truth, concise in all its parts and tells everyone what life really consists of and how to live it.

Statements of the highest spiritual nature are uttered by the SUGMAD to Sat Nam to show that the Supreme Deity wants all Souls to be lifted into the heavenly realm again: "I am eternal, therefore, I am free. All who come unto Me shall experience freedom of eternity.

"Freedom is a completeness within itself, for Soul must enter into the Divine Light or suffer the effects of the lower reality.

"The true reality in any universe of Mine is Spirit, and he who looks upon It as giving him existence and experience is indeed a wise man."

The ancient books of the SHARIYAT-KI-SUGMAD are indeed the true Light and the Word of God: It takes up and discusses every phase of life in both the worlds of matter and the highest planes.

Those who are fortunate enough to be able to peruse its golden pages are indeed enlightened Souls. Usually, it is the Spiritual Travelers who make it their concern to study this golden book of wisdom and spread its light to those who will listen.

Indeed, as Rebazar Tarzs, the torchbearer of ECKANKAR in the world today, points out, only the courageous and adventurous in spirit ever have the opportunity to see and study its wondrous pages.

Whatever truth each of us may receive is only in accord with our individual consciousness.

One will find within these pages an answer to every question man has ever devised to ask of any greater ones. All that which is truth is here now, within these pages.

Paul Twitchell

1

The ECK—The Divine Voice of SUGMAD

ECK is the totality of all awareness. It is the omnipresence of the SUGMAD, the omniscience and the omnipotence, the allness of the divine SUGMAD in ITS kingdom and the universes.

Life is concerned only with the primal Vadan, the Word of IT. This is the essence of life. Nothing is greater than the Word of the worlds.

Hence the SUGMAD speaks to us only through the primal Sound. IT has no other way of contact other than through the ECK, the creative energy. Out of this Divine Voice all other sounds flow.

Those who are in It distinguish between the primal Word and the manifest worlds, between the original music and Its echo. They are able to point out the difference between the Dhunatmik Sound and the Varnatmik sounds.

The all-creative ECK is the Voice of the SUGMAD, out of which all other sounds arise. At the same time Its divine strains linger in all material planes as echoes of the original melody.

1

The Voice of the SUGMAD is the Dhunatmik, the Sound which cannot be spoken. It has no written symbol. Such is the music of the SUGMAD. The Varnatmik is the sound which can be spoken or written. Hence, the scriptures of the Shariyat-Ki-Sugmad can be spoken and written on the lower planes. But in the higher worlds it is only the heavenly white music.

The ECK is the Ocean of Love, a lifegiving, creative sea, heard by the divine followers of the SUGMAD. Within the Ocean of Love is the total sum of all teachings emanating from the SUGMAD. It is the Divine Word, for It includes everything that SUGMAD has said or done, and what IT is.

The Voice of the SUGMAD includes all the qualities of the magnificent Being in the Ocean of Love and Mercy. It is a continuous process, flowing down from Its place in the Celestial Kingdom into all worlds below.

This Ocean of Love and Mercy projects Itself in the form of waves emerging out of a fountain. Since It contains the qualities of the SUGMAD, It can only appear on the lower planes—including the physical—as a form of consciousness.

Hence, as It reaches the Soul, or Atma, Plane, It manifests Itself as Sat Nam, in Sach Khand. Here this divine Being becomes fully personified for the first time, manifesting all of the qualities of the SUGMAD.

Sat Nam becomes the personal creator, lord, god, and father to all who are religious followers. He is the source out of which the Voice, the Wave of the SUGMAD, flows to all worlds below.

ITS Voice may be heard and seen by those who are able to participate in It throughout the worlds of the supreme Deity. It may be seen and heard only by those awakened selves, who have received the initiation from the ECK Adepts.

When the human consciousness in one has been awakened and he hears and sees the Wave of the SUGMAD, he is the enlightened. He hears the SUGMAD, sees IT, and feels the omnipotency of IT, for the ECK is the divine Deity expressing ITSELF in all that is visible and audible.

The Wave of the SUGMAD'S Voice, issuing through Sat Nam, flows outwardly from the Ocean of Love and Mercy, reaching the vast boundaries of the spiritual worlds and of all creation. Then It flows back into the ocean again, as do the waves created by a pebble dropped in a still pond.

Moving on It, all power and all life appear to flow outward to the uttermost bounds of creation, and again on It, all life appears to be returning to Sat Nam. Therefore, it is the returning wave of the Voice that Soul must look to for help.

The ECK Adept makes the connection, and the individual Soul is linked with this returning wave. It is then that Soul, or Atma, again starts Its journey toward the heavenly worlds, leaving all the worlds of mortality behind.

Thus the SUGMAD will speak to those who are obedient to ITS Word, for IT holds all life within ITS hand. All shall have the Light and the Word if they listen to IT and obey.

The SUGMAD has little involvement with embodiments. ITS relationship is only with consciousness, striving toward a totality of awareness so that every Atma will recognize Itself as being one with the ECK.

The SUGMAD is omnipresent, omnipotent, and omniscient in all life, and IT desires to have every Atma share these qualities. He who listens and sees the living ECK will experience these Godlike qualities and may use each for the welfare of all concerned.

Hence, the supreme doctrine is the Voice of the

3

SUGMAD. He who follows the golden arrow and crosses the mighty moat of heaven, where within the deep ravine sparkles and shimmers the strange translucent mist, enters into the secret kingdom of the holy SUGMAD.

The Voice that calls him is that which beckons all to take the first step upon the path to pass through the narrow gate and receive the graces of the Holy of Holies. Only he who is pure of heart will be able to partake of the arcane ecstasy, and become aware of the divine ground of Being.

Within the Temple dwells the SUGMAD. Unapproachable in ITS state except by the purest Atma, descriptions are unworthy of IT. The Atma can only experience the SUGMAD in the state of freedom. Those who are faithful will be free and able to live in the radiance of IT.

Fasting, eating certain foods, praying, beseeching, pleading, and the practice of austerities will never lead the Atma into the secret dwelling place.

The SUGMAD is engaged only with life and the Atma—never with forms, symbols, and objects. The Atma is immortal, cannot be injured, pierced, broken, wronged, drowned, or stolen.

The Voice speaks to all who listen. It speaks in the whisper of the wind, the roar of the sea, and the voices of birds and animals—in all things. It tells all who listen that It will never bring riches, fame, wealth, healing, or happiness to those who seek these mundane gratifications.

All who listen, obey, and surrender unto It shall have whatever is Its desire, be it riches, wealth, healing, happiness, enlightenment, or understanding of the divine wisdom.

The SUGMAD sends ITS messengers into this world as warriors. None come as doves. They are the eagles who must seek food for the young. They are the shepherds who keep the wolves away from the flock.

The Adepts for the ECK are the swordsmen of the SUGMAD. Whenever they travel, the pace of karma is quickened. In their wake comes the storm that divides nation against nation, and family against family. The elements of the wrath of the ECK bring down temples, demolish cities, and tear Souls asunder. It brings storms, floods, earthquakes, wars, and catastrophes.

Each Atma must fight Its battle against the storm of karma and the forces of the lower kingdom until victory is at hand. Then the realm of the SUGMAD is opened unto the victor.

The spiritually blind can never see the Light, nor the deaf hear the Voice of the SUGMAD. He who claims to be a master but is blind shall reap the harvest of wrath. The one who says he is a listener to the Voice but is deaf shall be torn asunder by his lying tongue.

The gods who are the messengers of the Divine Voice know and see the blind and the deaf. They know the liar, the questioner, and the deceiver. They know that these shall not see the face of the SUGMAD.

He who has the eyes to see shall view the Light of the ECK upon the face of the Mahanta. He who has the ears to hear shall gather unto himself the wisdom of the Voice of ECK within the worlds of the SUGMAD!

He who must know and see and hear shall be the perfect Soul. He has received purification and is ready to enter into the Heavenly Kingdom once again. He is an instrument and can talk with the Lord and be led by It.

Hence, wherever the Master goes wreckage follows. For he is always the instrument of ECK. The purification of ECK, the Voice of the supreme SUGMAD, causes the forces of the lower nature to cease. The cessation brings a warfare and, therefore, all know that life in the Pinda, or Physical, universe is a struggle between the spiritual

5

and physical.

Man, the apex of the Pinda universe, is often the conveyer of the seeds of Kal Niranjan, the negative power. The Kal and its children do battle with the ECK and Its children. The war is always between these two powers, resulting in victory for the ECK for those who desire it so.

Whosoever wants the life of the ECK must remember the falseness of the Kal. Soul must exist upon the essence of the ECK. The Voice that speaks must be that which leads the chela into the true home of the SUGMAD, the Ocean of Love and Mercy.

Therefore, Soul must know that life and love are not in the voice of the Pinda consciousness. Nor are they in the voice of the Nuri, or Astral, existence; nor in the Karan, or Causal, world; nor in the Manas, or Mental, world. Life and love are only in the world of ECK. Unless one hears that which we know as the Bani or the Nada Bindu, the seed Sound from which all things grow, he has heard only the voices of these other worlds.

The wolves who come in sheep's clothing will sing the praises of the voice of the lower worlds. Heed them not. Listen only to the messengers of the supreme SUGMAD. They who travel from the ECK to the regions of Jot Niranjan are like the prophets of old. They are the instruments that the SUGMAD uses to give ITS message to the universes.

The Voice is that Essence—the Holy Ghost, the Comforter, the Divine Spirit—that gives life to all. It has many names—Shabda, Logos, the Word, the Nada, Shabda Dhun, Akash Bani, Sultan-ul-Azkar, the King of the Ways, Ism-i-Azam, Kalma, Kalam-i-Illahi, Surat Shabda, Ananda Yoga, or Anahad Shabda. Others call It the Vadan, Dhun, the Heavenly Music, and other names.

Only those who follow the ECK Marg, the path of ECK,

know the truth that life consists of the Living ECK Master, the Bani, and Jivan Mukti, which is spiritual liberation in this lifetime. This is the way man leaves the Pinda and finds his way to heaven again. All must go this way. He might go another way, but the Marg is then slower. When his persevering efforts have brought him victory, he shall have the perfectly clear understanding that all he can do for himself is useless unless he accepts the way of ECK.

When one has definitely stripped off the Pinda values, then the ECKshar, the state of Self-Realization Consciousness, will burst forth, and the heavenly music will bring ecstasy. Upon this encounter he will find that there is no path, for there is no place to go. All is eternity. He is at the unique and the fundamental center of All.

This is Jivan Mukti!

This is the deliverance, the disappearance of the illusion of servitude, because of man's unhappy conduct toward man. This freedom takes away his blindness and opens his eyes. It takes away his deafness and opens his ears. He proceeds, with the help of the Living ECK Master, the Vi-Guru, who is the Spiritual Traveler, to receive his initiation into the holy ECK. Then all things are made whole again.

Thus he knows that the modus operandi is not the cause which precedes all form; It is only the instrument through which the First Cause operates.

He who looks upon the face of the mighty SUGMAD will never again be the same. He will thereafter be like the lion upon the trail of the deer. Hunger will drive him to the ECK Marg, and he will find the Holy Spirit in time, be it through the help of the Master, the Son of Heaven, or by his own way. But be aware, for he will find It.

Be on guard, lest he who seeks without the Vi-Guru, the Supreme Guru, find those who only appear as the Holy One, claiming to be angels or saints. Let none

7

deceive the chela. If he who seeks is a chela of the Vi-Guru, he cannot be deceived by the Kal Niranjan. If he has not the armor of Spirit, he can be misled.

The Kal is treacherous, and the lower worlds are filled with those who desire to be recognized as great deities. A vision may be the creation of the manas. Man spends much of his time viewing creations of the mind manas. Such creations are not reliable communicants. Without the clear vision of the Vi-Guru—he who is the Master—and the tests given by him, one cannot be assured of what he sees or hears.

Every Spiritual Traveler, or Vi-Guru, will give the Word to the chela to call upon the Master. If the vision fails to reply then it is false. He cannot see the holy Light, nor hear the holy Sound. He is the blind and the deaf whose eyes and ears are sealed until the Traveler arrives to unseal them.

Upon arrival in the worlds of true Spirit, there is no path on which to travel, no door to open, there is no gate, there is nowhere to go because there is no need to go anywhere. This is the wonderful secret of the SUGMAD.

The SUGMAD is within every man, but due to ignorance, man is always seeking IT on the outside; seeking ITS Word in the noises of the Pinda kingdom.

It is true that the Word, the Voice of the SUGMAD, is difficult to hear, but it is easy to submit the Self to those who have It. It has always been the case that all have not received the Word, and yet they had the protection of the Travelers. Surrender to the Master, who is the instrument of the ECK, is the great pleasure of life. This path of surrender is only used by those who are mortals. He who is mortal must follow the way of submission.

Man must give himself to the Holy Spirit of the SUGMAD. He must let the Voice of Silence lead him into the heavenly worlds. If he who follows the Bani be brave,

8

there shall be victory; but if he be fearful, only death of the mortal self shall result. Beyond this death of the Pinda Sarup, the physical body, there shall be nothing for him. He shall live in darkness and ignorance until the Vi-Guru sees him and has compassion on his suffering.

If the Vi-Guru looks upon mortal man with compassion in his eyes, that mortal shall be given the instant way into heaven. He shall find himself caught up in the twinkling of an eye into the Ocean of Love and Mercy. When the Vi-Guru turns his head aside and passes on, the mortal shall continue his life suffering until he learns to ask the Saint to show him the way out of the Pinda world.

Love comes to one in whom the Word has stirred. It is like the rushing of the mighty winds and the tongues of fire.

This message of love is translated from the Word of the SUGMAD to all the universes and to every living being. It is the message that is given to all entities living on every plane of the spiritual universes by the Living ECK Master of the highest Order. It is the difference between the recorded scriptures and the ECK.

It glorifies the living Master and gives to those who ask the Crown of Life—the holy Initiation into ECK, approved by the Living ECK Master. No chela is ready for the initiation until he has undergone the trials of the cave of fire, and the water test. These are all encountered on the path of ECK, before reaching that spiritual level of initiation.

Thereafter, the chela enters into glorious life with the SUGMAD. But until then he will be blown before the wind like the chaff of wheat scattered over the fields. He will suffer the agonies of spirit until the burden seems too great, and all is lost. He will drown himself in tears and pleas to the SUGMAD to give him amity and rest.

But it will appear that the divine Deity has turned ITS face away and the Living ECK Master has forsaken him.

He will yearn for peace and tenderness but none will be forthcoming. All hope will die within him, and he will feel that his life is unworthy of anything but the Kal Niranjan, the prince of darkness and materiality.

The Godman does not come into this world to make new laws, nor to destroy existing laws, but only to uphold the Universal Divine Law, unchangeable as it is. His message is one of hope, fulfillment, and redemption for those in search of the SUGMAD. He is a great cementing force, transcending all denominational creeds and faiths and presenting a way out of the worldly religious strongholds.

He travels high into the ethereal atmosphere of the spiritual worlds and like the skylark establishes an abiding link between the mundane life on earth and the pure spiritual heaven. All religions are subject to the Godman's love and yet none shall bind him, for he gives to all humanity what is essentially sublime for every individual Soul.

The gulf that separates the pontifical heads on one hand and a truly God-intoxicated Soul on the other is vast. The God-intoxicated Soul who is the Living ECK Master combines in his person all that the scriptures contain and much more besides.

He is the living embodiment of all that is religious, the spirit of life lying dormant in others. He is the awakened Soul, transcending time and space and causation, holding the past, present, and future in the palms of his hands as an open book. He is the Master of the creative life impulse throbbing in all things, visible and invisible, and is able to work simultaneously on all planes—Physical, Astral, Causal, or Mental, and even beyond into the supreme worlds of the Anami.

He is the Word made flesh, as spoken of by St. John the Apostle, and dwells among all races to gradually lead the aspiring Soul back to the eternal Godhead, from plane to plane with varying degrees of density. The ECK teachings, which he gives, promise a practical way out of the dense matter into the pure spiritual sunshine. The ECK, or Word, manifests in the Master and is revealed to those whom he may so choose to call his own.

His experience is a direct Soul manifestation unlike those who work on the intellectual plane and quote scriptures in support of what they preach.

The only reason the Godman uses the scriptures is to correctly explain and interpret the spiritual experiences of Soul on Its journey homeward, in addition to the actual, practical inner events granted to individuals. Thus he leaves no room for doubt and skepticism.

All knowledge one has at this point is based upon sense-perception or is derived from intellectual ratiocination. The knowledge that the true, living Master gives is direct and immediate, coming from actual Soul experiences apart from the physical senses and human consciousness. His words are charged with the ECK currents surging within him. They sink into the inner self of the listener, leaving little doubt about the existence of Soul experiences.

ECK is the golden thread, so fine as to be invisible yet so strong as to be unbreakable, which binds together all beings in all planes, in all universes, throughout all time and beyond time into eternity.

Since the first flicker of consciousness dawned on human intelligence this thread was there, and it caused man to probe into the depths of himself to learn about the experiences of the inner life. Man is older than religions, but not older than ECK, for It predates all life on earth. It was in the beginning and the ending of all things,

11

and is what sustains us in the present. Its very presence is the essence of the SUGMAD.

Thus man's being older than religions but younger than the ECK has caused him to wonder about this golden thread of life, and he has begun to look for the answers to the riddle of life. In the end he will learn that all religions established so far throughout the world have their origin in the Godman, the Living ECK Master who comes to this world, lives among humanity, and guides all footsteps to the Kingdom of God. Every religion in this world is a living testimony to this sacred truth.

The natural way back to God is known as ECKANKAR, the Ancient Science of Soul Travel, which is an exact science embracing the purest of the original teachings. It is the original of itself and its simplicity, once grasped, is staggering to the intellect. It is the most ancient of all teachings, known to us in its earliest form through the Naacal writings, which are hidden in the Katsupari Monastery in northern Tibet under Fubbi Quantz. It is the original fountain from which all faiths spring.

It is the same basic truth which Yaubl Sacabi expressed so concisely during his time on earth many centuries ago in a few powerful words: "The SUGMAD is the essence of everything within us." Herein lies the key. There is nothing vague or complex in this statement, nothing which cannot be applied to all persons living in the physical world. Yet few people are able to step through the tenth door which leads Soul into the heavenly worlds. This is the basic principle of ECK. Heaven exists in all persons, and all persons have access to It.

All religions teach that God is within, but this is not true. It is not God, the SUGMAD, that is within every Soul, but the essence of God, or that known as the ECK.

The methods of ECKANKAR state explicitly how to find this state of consciousness which exists within Soul.

The road leading to this state, which is the Kingdom of Heaven, starts behind the eyes at a point between the eyebrows. This is the tenth door, which leads Soul to the original heavenly home from which It started eons ago. When all consciousness is withdrawn from the body to focus at this point then the marvelous journey of Soul begins.

The human body does not have to die to make these journeys to God. Each visit will be only temporary until one leaves the body for the last time on earth. This is the art of death in life. The meaning of this was brought forth when Rami Nuri, the great ECK Master in charge of the Shariyat-Ki-Sugmad in the House of Moksha in Retz, the capital of Venus, said, "He that wants life badly will never have it, but he that gives it up for the ECK, shall have all life."

This is the true meaning of the death-in-life struggle, for once life is given up to serve only the ECK, he who does so becomes blessed. Truth is manifested when one seeking God wants to be shown the supreme Deity, for he has only to look upon the Living ECK Master to fulfill this desire. Gopal Das once stated that "whoever has looked upon the face of the Godman has seen the living image of God." This means the Living ECK Master has been sent to this world to serve and act for the highest reality. He has been sent by the Divine Power to administer to all who need him during his sojourn on earth.

"Those who follow the ECK take nothing for granted, for they must prove it for themselves. Only then will they know that God so loved them that He sent a Living ECK Master to bring Souls home to Him," Gopal Das said, repeating the words from the Shariyat-Ki-Sugmad.

The chela must prepare for the journey back to God. The way is a narrow footpath, and it is best to leave all baggage behind for it is filled with desires and

13

attachments. The chela must cast off the yoke that weighs him down. But the chela keeps asking himself, "Am I worthy of God?"

No one is worthy of God. It is only through the Grace of the supreme SUGMAD that we become worthy. Only the Living ECK Master can bring this Grace to those who seek IT, for he is the pure instrument of God on earth. So we must keep our faith with the Living ECK Master and live in his presence as much as possible.

In prehistoric times man took an enormous leap upward from the animalistic life with the development of consciousness. Now ECK is giving the human race the opportunity to take another equally great step upward into Cosmic Consciousness. The effect will enable man to make more spiritual progress by this second step than he made materially through the first.

The SUGMAD is what there is and all there is, so that no name can really be given IT except the poetic name of God. IT is neither old nor new, great nor small, shaped nor shapeless. Having no opposite, IT is what opposites have in common; IT is the reason why there is no white without black and no form apart from emptiness. However, the SUGMAD, as we know IT, has two parts—an inside and an outside. The inside is called Nirguna, which is to say that IT has no qualities and nothing can be said or thought about IT. The outside is called Saguna, which is to say that IT may be considered as eternal reality, consciousness, and joy. This is the part that man knows and remembers after experiencing the God-Realization state.

Because of Its joy in reaching this state, Soul is capable of enjoying Itself in play. This type of play is called Lila and is like singing and dancing made up of sound and silence, motion and rest. In this kind of play, Soul will lose Itself and find Itself in a game of hide-and-seek without beginning or end. This is the joy that the orthodox religions speak about, but in the losing of Itself, It is obliterated; It forgets that It is the one and only reality and plays that It is the vast multitude of beings and things which make up this world. In finding Itself, It is remembered; It will discover again that It is forever the one behind the many, the trunk from which the branches of the tree grow—the tree itself. It knows again that Its seeming to be many is always maya, or illusion, art and magical powers.

The play of Soul is like a drama in which Soul is both the actor and audience. On entering the theater the audience knows that it is about to see a play, but the actor creates maya, an illusion of reality which gives the audience extreme emotions of joy or terror, laughter or tears. It is in the joy and sorrow of all beings that Soul, as audience, is carried away by Itself as the actor.

Among the many images of God is the Hamsa, the divine bird, which lays the world in the form of an egg. It is also the syllable *ham* that God breathes out, scattering all galaxies in the sky. With the syllable *sa* IT breathes in, withdrawing all things to their original unity. The syllables *ham-sa* may also be heard as *sa-ham*, or *sa-aham*, which is to say, "I am THAT," or "THAT Soul"—what each and every being *is*. Breathing out, God is called in the lower worlds by the Sanskrit name of Brahma, the Creator. Holding the breath out, God is called Vishnu, the Preserver of all these lower worlds. Breathing in, God is called Shiva, the Destroyer of maya, or illusion.

This is the ancient truth without beginning or end. Soul is sent into the worlds of matter where It loses Itself and finds Itself. It always lives in various forms, in periods known as days and nights. Each day and each night lasts for a Kalpa, which is four and a quarter million, (4,320,000) of our years. The day, which is known as

15

Manvantara, is divided into four yugas, or epochs, which are named as in the throws of the game of dice—the first is Krita, or Satya; the second, Tretya; the third, Dwapara; the fourth, Kali.

Krita, or Satya, yuga is the Golden Age, the era of total delight in multiplicity and form and every beauty of the sensuous world. It endures for 1,728,000 years. Tretya Yuga is a shorter era which lasts for 1,296,000 years and is that period when everything starts to go amiss and every pleasure has some anxiety attached. Dwapara Yuga is shorter than these. It runs for 864,000 years, and in it the forces of light and darkness, good and evil, pleasure and pain are equally balanced. Last comes the Kali Yuga, lasting for 432,000 years, in which the universe is over-whelmed by darkness and decay, and Soul is lost in a delight which is hardly more than a disguise of horror. The form of Shiva takes place here, and the universe is turned to ashes and nothingness. This is when the Lord SUGMAD takes up all Souls to the Soul Plane, the fifth world, and destroys the lower regions in fire and ashes.

Souls who have been transplanted to this upper region find themselves in original unity and bliss. They remain in this Kalpa of 4,320,000 years in a life of total peace, before the cycle starts again and they are returned to the new worlds of matter.

As God breathes out, the worlds are manifested. These worlds are not our own earth planet, nor those planets and stars in the sky, but the worlds we cannot see that are hidden in the body of the tiny ant or bee. The stars of our heavenly world can be contained in the eyes of a swallow. There are also worlds around man that do not respond to our five senses, worlds which are great and small, visible and invisible, and as numerous as the grains of sand on the seashore.

These worlds are levels of consciousness. They are made

manifest by the Lord SUGMAD, and it is the divine purpose that all beings pass through these worlds at some time or other. Each Soul will pass through what is the twelve paths, or divisions, of the Wheel of Becoming. This is the Wheel of Eighty-Four, which goes the complete round of the Zodiacal circle. It is here that Soul spends eighty-four lacs in each Zodiacal sign, and each lac is equivalent to one hundred thousand years. Eighty-four lacs amount to eight million four hundred thousand years.

A wandering Soul, making Its way from birth to birth, may possibly be required to pass Its long and tiresome course through all these signs of the Zodiac, provided Its karma calls for it. But there is an escape, and that is to meet with the Living ECK Master and accept him. The Master will link him to the ECK stream of Life and there do not have to be further births for him. He is now free of the Wheel of the Eighty-Four.

He will reach that place where he is no longer desirous of the fruits of action, as all within the lower worlds are seeking action motivated by desire for results, whether good or evil. This binds them to the Wheel of Becoming by their karma. Each will stay bound to it as long as their ignorance is prevalent and as long as none meet with the living Godman. Each must come to that position or level of spiritual understanding in which he knows that, "I have come to be, and I shall cease to be," in the words of the ECK Master, Peddar Zaskq.

One must set aside all ideas, opinions, theories, and beliefs and look earnestly and intently at the one great principle of ECK, the "I AM." Whosoever does this will find himself awakened by the knowledge of the divine Self, that there is no other center of the ECK than himself. Thus he is liberated while still in the human form, before the death of the body, and before the dissolution of all worlds at the end of the Kalpa. He has reached the state of Jivan Mukti, liberation of Soul via the Sound Current.

On all sides, within and without, he sees all beings, all things, all events, as only the playing of the Lord SUGMAD in ITS myriad forms. He has become the Co-worker with the SUGMAD and cannot do other than the will of the Divine, for his will has become that of the highest. He no longer uses the terms, "my Soul" or "your Soul," for now he knows he is Soul Itself and must at all times see from this specific viewpoint.

No one shall reach these joyous heights of Spirit unless he has been trained in the works of ECKANKAR. A specific attitude and viewpoint is necessary for the satisfactory utilization of the spiritual powers; he who uses them must be free from emotional bias and entirely detached and serene in his attitude. Otherwise, he will be a failure at traveling the path to God.

A knowledge of mechanics is not at all necessary for the spiritual works of ECKANKAR; it is the attitude that is all important and that determines the nature of the ultimate issues of God. This attitude can only be arrived at by self-discipline and purification of Soul.

Thus the greater ceremonial rituals of the initiation into ECK are unsuitable for the use of anyone save a trained initiate. But there are many minor rites that can be used by anyone who achieves a steady mind. Knowledge is secondary to all things in the spiritual works except for the issues at hand, to know whether it is right or wrong to take a specific course.

Every decision in life depends upon the factors that lie behind it. The Physical Plane, as the spiritually awakened man sees it, is the end result of a long chain of evolutionary processes that have gone on in the more subtle planes, the realms of the Soul, Mental, Causal, and Astral planes. Consequently, every problem of human nature, every decision that man makes on the Physical Plane, will have a magnetic field of its own, an aura composed of factors from each of these levels of consciousness. The initiate realizes this, because every action is composite. He must determine the relative proportion of these different factors and discern upon what level the action has its nucleus.

When man comes into the state of Soul Consciousness, he realizes that each plane of existence has its own laws and conditions, and that these cannot be overridden by any power, however great, except by the will of the Godman. Each plane exists because of the one above it, to the extent that the powers and mechanisms can be adjusted and directed to its own conditions. Only the living Godman has power to bend any circumstances, conditions, and laws of any of the planes within the universes of God. He seldom does this, nevertheless he has the authority, for he is the manifestation of the Lord SUGMAD upon this plane and every plane within the worlds of worlds.

Man cannot change anything in life, but his own ego tells him that it is possible. These are only the false whispers of Kal Niranjan, the king of the lower worlds, in order to hold Soul and trap It there. As quickly as man learns that his powers are puny, the sooner will he put his feet upon the path to God by the way of ECKANKAR. As soon as this is done, he will find himself being led by the Living ECK Master, who has taken over to assist him in reaching his true home again.

19

2

The ECK Sastras

To understand the SUGMAD, the Lord of all universes, is to understand nothing. That known as the SUGMAD is the Allness of life, the fountainhead of Love and Mercy, to be named with any name you wish.

Spiritual essence is based upon the Mahanta, the inner form of the Living ECK Master. This is the radiant form, often called the Nuri Sarup, which gleams like a thousand stars in the night. Until the chela is able to view and speak with the Mahanta, and to travel with him in the worlds of spiritual life, he is without true realization.

To understand the SUGMAD, in the very beginning it is best to understand the Mahanta, the living Godman. This is the affirmation and declaration of the SUGMAD, involving neither denial nor negation but a placing of full belief in the Mahanta to know what God might be. ECK is the true path, and Its own spiritual practices laid down by the Mahanta lead to true knowledge of the SUGMAD.

---

*Sastras: scriptures

21

Man should know that in Soul there is being, knowing, and seeing. In the mind there is nothing more than thought, volition and analysis, while in the body there is only action.

All who become the channel for God will translate the ECK into the physical and spread peace to those concerned. Mind is the intermediate link between heaven and earth; therefore, it is good to use the mind as an instrument, allowing the spirituality of God to flow to all living creatures. Being an instrument of God, one asks not for solace, but only to give solace; one asks not for peace, but to give peace; and one asks not for happiness, but seeks only to give happiness.

The lives of the saints from the ancient Order of the Vairagi remind man that everyone can make his life sublime, while in the flesh. There is no mystery for him to seek, for all is as clear as the morning sun. Man must awaken and rise, tread the path of ECK carefully and with perseverance until he has reached the great goal, with no thought of rest.

If you aspire after truth, come, follow the Mahanta; practice the Spiritual Exercises of ECK, experiment and realize the purport of the divine teachings. Do not praise nor condemn the works of ECK until Its truth is realized.

Man is a creature, but so is the god who rules the universes of matter. This god is the binding principle, whom those in ECK designate as the Kal, or Maha Kal. He is the supreme deity of all the known regions of the physical universe. Bound as he is, he binds all.

The idea of bondage comes from him and his Ahankar. He is the ruler of the spirito-material worlds, and as long as the unawakened Soul finds Itself inhabiting the realm of Kal, It cannot dream of release from the fetters of the Kal that decrees all Souls should remain bound. It is the will and the struggle of Soul to become free.

Ordinarily Soul is confined to the planes of the lower worlds—the Physical, Astral, Causal, Mental, and Etheric, or the subconscious. It is also confined in the fetters of a three-conditioned consciousness called wakefulness, dream state, and dreamlessness. While encased in the bounds of the lower worlds, Soul has to be content with living in these conditions of Kal.

The awakened Soul, though, performs Its functions in the spiritual worlds while living in the physical state. This is the being that lives within the physical body. It is here that he enjoys the foods of his senses, the body functions, and that which comprises life upon this plane of the material universes. This is the manner and life of the ECK chela, for he takes all within this life and enjoys it, knowing that he is dead here and will not be fully alive until the body dies. Nevertheless, he does not reject the experiences of the physical senses and the body.

The Atma, living in the dream consciousness of the psychic states, enjoys the subtle things of life, as thought, emotional joy, intellect, and mind stuff. All this is essential for the bodies of the psychic worlds, the Astral, Causal, and Mental planes. When Soul takes mastery over these states through dreaming, It becomes the supreme ruler of Its own universe.

The third state possesses neither wakefulness nor dreams. It is absorption in the state of being I AM! There is a consciousness of self-knowing, that the Atma has become an inhabitant of the world of Sat Nam. All the bodies the Atma has used on the planes of the worlds below are at rest, are in a dreamless, sound sleep. But the Atma is full in Itself, wise, and all-knowing about Itself. It enjoys the ecstasy of this high world and has the power to move wherever desired, to any plane of God below or above.

All existing life sprang out of the ECK, and exists only

by the presence of the ECK. In the beginning there was nothing but the ECK, the Word of the SUGMAD; unmanifested It was, and thence It arose into manifestation. The power within the ECK was polarized, and from It the vibrations of the ECK proceeded gradually, and innumerable worlds rushed forth into life and shape, as do bubbles rising from the bottom of a deep spring in globular forms.

Motion and action are always in the form of a curve, and from these curvilinear motions, or vibrations, were created spheres upon spheres in the psychic worlds below the Soul Plane.

The ECK is rooted and grounded in all life—he, she, it, I, thee and thou. It is here, there, and everywhere; permeating all directions, east, west, south, and north; above and below; everywhere, in all seasons. All personalities and impersonal things have their existence in the ECK. The ECK is the symbol of individuality, the Sound and the Light. It is the music of the spheres, the light of lights. It is the theories and practices of all things. The creator, creation, and creatures are only the ECK.

Some scriptures describe the ECK as the Word, the Ego principle permeating the universes. It is all that and something more as well. All that is, that will be, and that was, is nothing but the ECK. All find expression in the ECK, the Word. All is manifested in the ECK and by the ECK. All are represented by the ECK. It is explicable. It is inexplicable. It is the personification of the SUGMAD. It is the essential whole and the essential part of the SUGMAD speaking and giving life to all life. It is divisible and indivisible, limited and unlimited, thought and no-thought, visioned and unvisioned; these are nothing but the ECK. It exists as the very essence in the motor and sensory currents of the physical, and in the mental and thought faculties as the very heart of each, and their existing life. It is the cause of all actions and deeds, and is the effect of all causes.

Thus, the ECK is the creative principle proceeding by agitation of motion in the polarized throne of the SUGMAD throughout the worlds and universes. It pervades everything, for nothing can exist without the ECK. As threads in cloth are woven and interwoven, as the particles of water fabricate the sea, all things in the spiritual worlds and all things in the material worlds are woven and fashioned of the ECK. All in existence, whether entire or in parts, is the ECK only.

ECK is the embodiment of all attributes of life, of spiritual enlightenment, of vitality and vibrancy. It is endowed with intelligence as opposed to *Jad*, or materialism, and is the principle which finds expression in the word *Chaitanya*, which in Sanskrit embraces all things noted here.

The ECK descends and ascends in vibratory currents, producing life in all forms; producing music inherent and inborn that gives joy to the heart of those who have the power to hear Its melody. The middle aspect of ECK is Light, and Its lower aspect is intelligence. It vibrates and reverberates through all worlds. Within the higher worlds It creates the Sound, the music of life; within the psychic worlds It creates Light, and in the worlds of matter It creates intelligence.

All in all, It creates, sustains, and gives freedom to that chela who is able to hear the Music of the SUGMAD, to see the Light of the worlds and to know with the intellect. With this comes freedom, the liberation that brings to Soul the very essence of happiness. This is the true freedom, the true happiness, and the true knowledge of God.

The liberation of Soul from Its gross body is the freedom which man has sought for centuries, in each reincarnation, millions and millions of times repeated. Ever hoping to find perfection in some path to God, but never succeeding until he reaches and accepts the Mahanta. That perfection within him is recognized by the Mahanta; he is taken under the Mahanta's protection as the hen takes the baby chick under its wing to keep the world from crushing it.

By his nature, man can only grasp a particle of the totality of the SUGMAD by knowing and experiencing the God-state, but can also realize IT even more fully by directly linking up with Truth in such a way that the knower and the known are one. This is possible because human consciousness is dual. Man has two selves: the human ego, the self of which he is primarily conscious, considered erroneously as his real self; and the non-phenomenal self, the Real Self, the eternal Atma, the divinity within him. It is possible for man, if he so desires and is prepared to make the necessary effort and sacrifice, to realize and identify himself with the Atma Sarup. In doing this he is identified with, and comes into, the true knowledge of the totality of the SUGMAD.

Man must know that when he seeks God, he cannot find IT. He must know that he cannot touch God. Nor can his mind exceed IT. But when he no longer seeks God, then IT becomes a recognized part of himself; IT is always with him. He will come to know that God is a reality that has always been with him and has never left him; he cannot see IT because IT is hidden by the external senses that are used to see the world. These senses are not available in the inner world, for they have no use beyond matter. The inner senses are able to see all the outer world and the inner world. It is only by the use of the inner senses that the chela can find God, never by seeking IT with the outer equipment.

When man comes to apprehend things as they really

are, and not as they seem to be to his limited perception, then he can know God. Not only will he then enter into the state of being, but he will enter into the immortality of the Atma and be transformed. He will become the Kitai, the enlightened one. This is the second stage of initiation on the path of ECK.

Reality is One, though religions call it by various names. This is what the sages have said to be One in asserting the interiority of divinity in Soul. This inner essence, the spark of divinity which is of the SUGMAD, is always hidden, for It exists at a higher level of human life as the potential of God in man. For It to become truth, there must occur the divine birth, the actual realization within Soul. It is then that man is raised to the Kingdom of God.

The language of man cannot truly begin to describe the sacred worlds of God, only the language of the senses can. His speech cannot be that of a spiritual Volapuk, a silent one, capable of expression without limits, but is limited and contained in a space-time continuum. The man who can express his experiences in the realm of God does so by his deeds and shining countenance, not by words alone.

The ECK is not contained in space-time measures for It is out of space and time, and different in kind and degree from the worlds out of which the language of man is fashioned to describe the experiences of the senses. Thus the Mahanta can only describe the glories of the SUGMAD in an environ of polarity with a language of opposites—nonpersonal and personal, supernatural and natural, subjective and objective, without and within. Each is truth within its various spheres, within the different levels of significance and awareness; but none, alone or combined, can express complete truth. The truth found in God is without opposites, while the conflicts of time and space are ever present in the worlds of physical phenomena.

The SUGMAD, like freedom, must be won and rewon many times for freedom is an elusive element within the physical realms. This freedom is the ultimate reality of life, the ultimate result accumulated over the millions of incarnations of Soul on the physical plane. Upon meeting with the Mahanta, the acolyte, the seeker of God, becomes the chela. The Living ECK Master is the SUGMAD manifested upon earth and designated to gather up all Souls that are ready and take them into the heavenly worlds again. He who is willing and voluntarily gives up his life for the sake of the ECK is taken up to the glories of God now. He gains freedom within a flash, yet as long as he is in the temple of flesh he will have to win his way back into heaven many times without ceasing, never giving up in the face of hardships and suffering which the Kal Niranjan lays upon him while he lives in this world. So he who will lay down his life for ECK will gain life everlasting, life eternal.

The only way the chela can attain peace of heart and rid himself of all burdens of karma is through the ECK. By his own efforts to leave this worldly state of consciousness and travel into the realms of the SUGMAD can a purified vessel, a channel for God, live in this world of matter while at the same time dwelling in the timeless spheres.

Understanding is without form and must be used. The chela must realize this for he seeks, for the most part, in the outer worlds, the arena of matter, space, and time. The realization that understanding is a human means for gathering and storing impressions and experiences in the physical world brings Soul to the SUGMAD and the old knowledge of the spiritual realm. Only the single-minded actualizes his true potential and understands that understanding is for himself. It is not the same for all Souls, but differs with each.

There is no way to the SUGMAD except through the Mahanta. This is the greatest understanding that Soul may reach, but it must be direct knowledge, and not given him by another. So it is found that in Soul there is no ultimate knowledge but of Itself. This is what is sufficient for Soul and gives It immortality. Therefore, any speculation or philosophy about the SUGMAD is useless and meaningless for the human consciousness because IT cannot be seen, heard, nor reasoned.

The only way the human state can express God, speak of IT, or describe IT, is in relation to the Kal. The lower element will not allow the essence of God to come through clearly to human minds. God can force ITS own way, but only in dire cases of necessity will the SUGMAD express ITSELF in this world. This condition endures until the human element is conquered and Soul becomes One with One, when the two natures—the human and the divine—are united. This is when the Divine overcomes the worldly self and makes ITSELF known in the physical state. Few, if any, can find this state; fewer still ever solve the problem and attain this higher spiritual state of the supernatural life.

The state of God-Realization—attainment of the higher spiritual state of the supernatural life—is realized only in the personal aspect. This aspect is hinted at in all religions of the world. The idea of the SUGMAD as both impersonal and personal in ECKANKAR is expressed in the distinction noted between the ultimate Godhead, which is attributeless, and the Mahanta, whose characteristics include the Trinity.

Those who have earned the titular distinction of Mahanta serve their time in this world as the Living ECK Master, to gather up Souls and return them to their original home, the God-realm. For it was there they were created in Soul form and sent forth into the lower worlds along the grand circle route to take on the body form, life after life, until they eventually attained the spiritual awareness to recognize the Mahanta. He brings them into this world, and has been with them ever since their first birth into the spheres of time, matter and space. Few ever recognize the Mahanta, until they reach that certain position on their long journey through time and space when the scales fall from their eyes and he is seen in all his light and glory.

All earthly religious leaders fail with the majority, because they are not able to explain with precision the way of God. Few, if any, know the way of ECK. If they do, fewer still know it in a way to get it across to those who are hungering for the worlds beyond. Whosoever tries to explain the ECK without true experiences in the God-realm will not succeed. Whosoever shall have the opportunity to give and to teach ECK with experiences in God shall be successful.

He who has not been in tune with the ECK applies his knowledge to the pursuits of temporary gains and sensuous enjoyment, but the more spiritual realize that body and mind are but the outer and inner garments of Soul. The ignorant continually find themselves in touch with Kal at the lower level, while the spiritually enlightened find themselves in touch with the ECK at the higher level.

Soul is identified with the ECK, the essence of God, for Soul is that divine part of God which dwells in every man. The vibration of the solar sound unveils the true objective of Kal, but the Sounds of ECK reveal the divine reality of God within man.

It is only with the help of the Mahanta that the chela can come to such a spiritual level of awareness that he can differentiate between the state of phenomena and the knowledge of the noumenon. Thus the ECK is a self-manifesting power independent of living forms. All living forms are composed of It, and all living forms are nothing without It.

ECK functions in the consciousness, the life states, and the embodiment of forms in cohesive unity because of the ties of love that unite them. This is not the same love as we find existing between human states of consciousness. The latter type involves love and death, for whosoever shall love another in the human state shall find death. Love should not be given in the human state from one to another unless it is done in a disinterested way. This distinct human love always destroys, while the superior spiritual love gives increasing life. The ECK forms the consciousness in man, and spiritual love lifts and unites Soul with God. This is at once an impersonal and universal action, and those who have reached this state are known as the Vairagi Masters.

The spiritually blind grope through life in unhappiness, fear, and uncertainty. Mentally paralyzed, they seek the false security of dogma, superstition, social approval, national and personal pride, and temporal honor. Living in the limited awareness of the intellect and in the sensuous state of the physical environment, their lives are darkened by a deplorable ignorance of the spiritual self and their inherent divinity.

It is the ECK that awakens man to full realization of his divine nature. Nothing else is capable of doing this. All those who seek this realization from the varied religions, cults, and isms will meet with failure. Only the ECK can transform the human state of consciousness into divine Self-Realization, and gradually lead Soul on to the God state.

To a man who has achieved Self- and God-Realization, all religions, all philosophies, become just so many paths leading to the ECK. Through any of them, the seeker of

31

God can reach the divine ECK, the immaculate path to the Ultimate Reality. To the man who has touched the robe of God there is no distinction of race or belief, no consciousness of nationality, and no religious difference. The ECK has cleared away all conflicts and oppositions from his mental processes.

Each created form of life, by its own nature, longs for the perfection of the SUGMAD. It yearns for its well-being in the spiritual worlds, not the material worlds. It aspires for the perfection of the Divine One, graciously brought about by ITS Grace.

The most perfect object of love is the SUGMAD, for ITS glory is shown only to those who are able to receive ITS revelations. IT is hidden from those who are entrapped in the snares of their own weaknesses and who, in the hands of Kal Niranjan, remain the docile captive.

The SUGMAD manifests ITSELF to the elect in this world in diverse ways, and these elect become the chosen people. Followers of the path of ECKANKAR are the chosen ones whom God has selected to return again to the heavenly realm and become ITS Co-workers. They are the fortunate ones, the triumphant who have gained victory over the wiles of Kal Niranjan and who will reach the heavenly worlds again.

This beyond lies on the far side of cosmic consciousness, yet IT is attainable to all who will make the effort to find IT. IT is the transcendent, so magnificent in ITS scope and greatness—in comparison with the material universes—that the ego, the other worlds, and all therein are but pretty things against ITS immeasurable, majestic background. IT supports the universal activity of life. IT embraces life with vastness, or rejects it from ITS infinitude.

The ECK is the path, and to walk it is the enduring and unchanging way. All other ways are changeable and not reliable, for they can lead one only to the upper psychic planes. ECK is the nonpersonal and the personal path which takes the chela into the heart of God. Whatever is possible for the chela will be found on the way that is the highest, the ECKANKAR way, and no one may trod this path unless he is escorted by the Mahanta.

The three aspects of the SUGMAD are different from the Trinity of Christianity and Hinduism, and also different from the Trikaya of Buddhism, since it covers all things in life. The triple aspects are the three bodies of the Mahanta.

First there is the absolute primordial, the eternal Mahanta, called the clear voice of God, which dwells in the heart of the Ocean of Love and Mercy. There is no way to compare this with anything in Christianity, Hinduism, or Buddhism.

Second is the body of glory; the ECK, the Cosmic Spirit, the Sound Current which is in all life, giving existence to all things.

Third is the body of manifestation, the transformation, the historical Mahanta. This is the Living ECK Master in every age, who is the Eternal One, the bodily manifestation of the SUGMAD.

The historical Mahanta is the bodily manifestation of the eternal Mahanta and is the aspect in which the Divine One becomes incarnate in human form. The historical Mahanta possesses the same qualities as the Divine One in ITS second aspect, and manifests them as far as they can be manifested within the limitations of human nature within a definite point of history.

Man must build upon the ECK, never on the Kal. When one is working with the Kal, he becomes paralyzed in his upward climb and is continually working on a destructive basis. Most Souls in the lower worlds are living in this sort of void. This is described by the Buddhists

33

as Nirvana, the Void that is so highly praised. The main principle of karma is based on the Kal power, on destruction.

It is an axiom of ECK that whosoever tries to serve humanity will be a failure, but he who is willing and serves God is always a success in life. Few realize that the man who says his great desire is to serve mankind is speaking from the level of the Kal forces. It is one of Kal Niranjan's greatest traps to make one feel he is serving his fellowman. All those who heal the physical and mental aspects of man, who bring prosperity to man, who seek after peace for mankind, are deceived by the Kal forces into believing that this is God's design and will.

He who believes in social reforms for man is doomed to the lower levels of the Astral world, for this is but the work of the emotional body, which is the Astral body, working under the direction of the Kal forces. When the chela's spiritual eyes are opened he begins to see that the vast majority of works labeled as social forces, such as poetry, art, and music, have been created by the mind and are the Kal works of the Astral Plane, not of the true spiritual worlds.

The Mahanta is the distributor of karma in this world and what he says is the word of the SUGMAD. All the Lords of Karma are under his hand and must do as he directs. Hence, ECKANKAR is the spiritual refuge for all Souls. All are under the Mahanta, although few recognize and accept him as the spiritual avatar of the age. The spiritual body of the Mahanta is always with all people at all times, and cannot be replaced because some religions have a different name for him.

He has been the spiritual head of the world since its creation, manifesting physically to different races at different periods of human history as the vehicle for the

SUGMAD in the form to which they are most accustomed and by the name familiar to them. If the people were Hindu, he has appeared as Krishna, Buddha, or Vishnu, so they would know him. He was Zeus to the Greeks; Jupiter to the Romans; Osiris, Amun, Re, and Aton to the Egyptians; Jehovah to the old Judeans; Ishtar to the Babylonians; Varuna to the Aryans; Jesus to the Christians; and Allah to the Muslims. He has appeared to all in every age of this world. He is the secret force behind world historical events. None can escape the SUGMAD, and none be higher in this world and other worlds than the Mahanta, the Divine One, who is the manifestation in body form of the eternal Mahanta.

The Mahanta will rebuild the temple and gather in the Souls who wander in darkness. He places before each Soul the two ways: the way of life, and the way of death. The moment comes when no man can resist the summons. Where can man escape death? There is no place he can go except to God, to escape death. He cannot escape death while he is in the physical state, for there is no charm against it.

The ECK of Itself is a whole sovereign state, a condition of spiritual thought bound together by the idealism and love of Its own peoples. The universes of the SUGMAD are complete with a hierarchy of highly evolved beings who govern all the worlds according to the laws of their own worlds, and in accord with the will of the SUGMAD. The only difference between the spiritual hierarchy and the structure of the governments of the physical world is that the SUGMAD is a monarch in ITS government of the worlds. IT rules singularly and by divine nature. There are no democratic principles found here, and we either live according to the Divine Laws or become rebels and resist. Then we suffer whatever results by dwelling in the world of matter and being a

35

subject of Kal Niranjan, king of the negative force.

When man is able to leave his physical state of consciousness and travel in the inner worlds, he comes to that state where he passes the beyond—and suddenly he finds there is no state of consciousness existing in such a place. He is beyond the Void of Buddhism, the Heaven of the Christians, and the world of No Thing of Jainism. He is in the state of pure Being, if there is a vocabulary capable of describing it. Language and sound fail him.

The whole fabric of mankind is in the prison of society and self. This is a tragic existence controlled by Kal Niranjan in life after life. The Kal is the prison warden, and those who attempt to escape are usually independent. They believe in God, are stubborn and rambunctious; yet they, too, enslave themselves ever more securely in the prison of the Kal.

Man is both an exile and a prisoner, and his blindness is a darker imprisonment still. The inescapable confinement of Soul within this world is due mainly to the religion It follows. The church has become man's illusion and comfort. He parades before all people as righteous and spiritual, but he is likened unto a rotten apple where the peel has a glossy shine but the inner part is filled with worms.

The physical infects the body, and the astral infects the body and mind. Both also infect the causal body. But then the physical will infect the body, the astral infect the physical, the causal infect the astral and body, and the mind will infect all.

In the relationships that men have with one another, it is found that the astral and the mental have the greatest vitiative effect upon others. Those who stir up the astral waves and create disturbances among the human races suffer terribly without knowing what they did or how they did it. This is the danger of the psychic worker in this world. Be aware and do not have anything to do with them, for your ignorance will not be acknowledged nor be a reason for mercy when you face the Judge of the Dead. Your record here is what it is and your next assignment, unless you are under the protection of the Mahanta, will bring about more lives and further hardships, as one who violated the laws of the SUGMAD.

The mind infected by the Kal acts as a channel for the negative agent and infects other minds. The Kal elements which pour through the mind into the minds of the other persons become a poison which spreads from the youth to the elderly. No one living in the human consciousness is ever free from this unless he is under the protection of the Mahanta. Age believes that it is triumphant because it has wisdom, but this is because the Kal wants the elderly to believe this; and the youth live in the rebellion of blindness because Kal has set its course this way. None are free unless they follow the path of ECK. Orthodox religion will not save them, but will enslave all who follow it. Philosophy will furnish only a balm and salve for those who want to follow this never-successful path.

The Mahanta is the messenger of the Absolute. There are none before him and there will be none after him. All those who come to him in the present age have been with him since their advent into the world. He has developed them to this state of spiritual development so that by now they have reached the level wherein their recognition of him is apparent. He is able to accept each chela for what he is, and then put his feet on the path to reach the state of God-Realization within this lifetime.

Not all chelas under the Mahanta will necessarily reach the state of either Self-Realization or God-Realization within this lifetime. Should the Mahanta leave this life in his physical form before he has completed his duty with them, he will reappear again here on earth in another body to finish his task. He comes again and again in every age to take up the task of salvation with every Soul that reaches out or has reached out to him in some life. His duties with each Soul never cease; he is to take each back into heaven to become the Co-worker with God. He has never left any Soul who has made contact with him, sometime, somewhere in the past, or in this life. Once Soul has made the slightest degree of contact with the Mahanta, there is never any parting between them. He becomes as close to his loved ones as their own heartbeat, as their own breathing.

The body of the Mahanta is the ECK. This is the essence of God which flows out from the Ocean of Love and Mercy, sustaining all life and tying together all life forms. This is the consciousness of God, the very fluid that man lives upon. It is the highest form of God energy, and the greatest level of consciousness. The body form is merely the vehicle through which the ECK flows to uplift all life which comes in touch with the world. Without the body of the Mahanta within the universes, things would wither away and die.

The Mahanta liberates Soul from the grasp of the Kal forces. He is the good that dwells in the heart of every mortal creature. He is the beginning, the lifespan, and the end of all mortal creatures. He is the radiant sun, the wind, the stars of the night, and the moon. He is the king of heaven, of the sense organs, of the mind, of the consciousness of living. He is the spirit of fire, the spirit of the mountains, leader of all priests, the ocean's spirit, the greater seer; the sacred syllable ECK, the tree, the ant, the thunder in the heavens, and the god of fishes and sharks. He is time and the eagle, the lion and bear, the rivers of the world, the sustainer, the newborn babe, and the old man preparing to die. In all things is his face, and in all life is he the divine seed. In this world, nothing animate or inanimate exists without him. This is the Lord SUGMAD in action, and one atom of ITS body sustains the worlds upon worlds. Not only is he the king of this world, but in all worlds, all planets, all planes.

Out of the shattering of man's image comes the death of his God, and with this comes the splendid vision of the worlds within worlds, bringing enlargement and release from this plane of flesh. No longer does the universe seem cold, impersonal and menacing, but aflame with the love of the SUGMAD. This vision is never superimposed upon another but rises out of the very texture of the cosmos. Man in his human state then begins to see it, only insofar as he has shattered the images of his past concepts of the SUGMAD.

The feeble denizen of this world feels as if he cannot trust himself to the ebb and flow of this immense spiritual universe. He needs to turn all his inner affairs over to the Mahanta until he can, on his own, be responsible for himself. He must know that despite appearances and the apparent evil flowing around him, he and everything else in it are safe. Freedom is impossible for one who does not recognize that the flow and ebb that pass through the Mahanta to the world are guaranteeing him a safe journey through the lower worlds. The state of spiritual knowing, what we name faith, is impossible if faith seems to conflict with reason and possibility. One cannot believe without tolerance and never can he believe in what he thinks impossible or unreasonable.

The experience of the Mahanta, as one knows him in the human flesh, is that of man, but the chela is to look at what is known as the two sides of the Mahanta. These are the human state and the spiritual body. There is the experience of the earthly man who walks and talks with his friends, who dies but rises again. There is the other experience of the spiritual ECK of the risen Mahanta, an experience of a divine indwelling of the SUGMAD immanent in man.

It is unreasonable to isolate or overstress the historical element in ECK, since to do so can result in failure to grasp the timeless significance of the Mahanta. Likewise, it is equally unreasonable to neglect or discard the ECK, for It is an essential part of the spiritual revolution taking place in every age, the constant conflict between the ECK and the Kal forces.

The idea of the Mahanta as representative man appears sometime to be quite startling to the traditionalists of religions. It need not be, though the eternal and essential Godman does involve seeming contradictions. The incarnation of the Mahanta in every age is not only a showing forth of the divine drama being played out, but also a continuing portrayal of the human drama. This gives the only true promise of salvation, the liberation of Soul from the world of matter.

3

The Doctrine
of the ECK Marg

In the beginning there was only the mighty SUGMAD, the Lord of Lords, the Absolute of all Absolutes, the All Holy of Holies, the All Merciful of Mercies, and the Omnipotent Omnipresence and Omniscient of all universes and worlds.

In the beginning, IT slept; stirring not in the Ocean of Love and Mercy in that sphere where man has never trod nor any angel dwelled. IT is not a land, nor place or abode, but a mighty ocean of splendor and love. IT is the reality of all realities, the dwelling place of the SUGMAD, the Ancient One whom all creatures, beings, and men have worshiped through the ages.

In the beginning IT was the Alpha that slept, but IT ruled in ITS slumbers over the mighty beings, elements, and creatures in the universes. Peace and happiness were everywhere, and little was there for the SUGMAD to concern ITSELF with over life and ITS offsprings. The sacred garden of esoteric wisdom in the Alaya Lok was delightful for those beings who amused themselves there, while the Almighty slumbered and dreamed new worlds.

In the eternity of the profound Ocean of Love and Mercy,

41

IT stirred and aroused ITSELF from this deep slumber. Wild tremors came down through the universes, shaking the heavens and those beings in the sacred gardens. They paused, then looked up in astonishment at the parting of the firmament. They were amazed at the seeming wrath of the heavenly world that split with rolling thunder and crashing echoes.

The SUGMAD aroused ITSELF and looked out over the vastness of ITS domain; saw only the creatures of ITS making in play, amusing themselves without giving to one another. IT whispered and the Word went forth into the worlds of worlds.

The worlds shook and all Souls flew to find safety, but none was to be found. They stood and trembled before the mighty SUGMAD, the God of all gods, and listened. "You have played when you needed to give succor and life to others; you must learn the Truth by dwelling in my mansions below. In the house of your Father! You shall return to my home when ready!"

None knew what the Voice of the Lord was saying. Yet all who heard ITS Voice wondered. IT was to build new worlds in which each Soul would spend Its youth, to germinate and spiritually unfold; to learn Its true nature and mission throughout the universes of God.

In the beginning all below the Atma world was only Spirit, that known as the ECK, which moved throughout the void. Everything was without life—calm, silent. Void and dark was the immensity of space and time. Only the supreme power, the ECK, the self-existing essence of the SUGMAD, moved within this dark gulf of nothing.

The desire came upon the SUGMAD to look upon this abyss outside the universes of Light and Sound. IT desired to create new worlds, and IT created these worlds below the Atma Plane. The desire came to IT to create the Zodiac and the twelve constellations therein, and to place living things upon each.

The desire came upon IT to form the Sun, Moon, planets, and other worlds of the void; and IT gave each thing life. In each was placed a different embodiment of flesh, but to the creation of Earth IT gave the apex of life, called man. But first there were only rude forms of life.

It took the gases, which were without form, and scattered them throughout all space. Out of them were formed the planes, universes, worlds and planets, including the Earth.

The gases solidified to form the worlds and all its heavens. Out of these came the water and the atmosphere; and darkness prevailed. There was no sound for, as yet the ECK had not entered into all the worlds of time and space.

After the atmosphere was created, the SUGMAD formed the outside gases and waters which covered the face of all worlds, and there were no land masses anywhere. So the SUGMAD looked and dreamed to see what IT would do with these worlds IT had created in the vast regions outside ITS own domain.

IT commanded the sun to give light and the atmosphere to open so that its rays could fall upon the worlds of darkness. Then light penetrated the darkness and made it bright and illuminated. The SUGMAD created the whirling masses in space and the planets began to rotate around the suns within their universes, including the Earth, and there was an alternating of light and darkness.

The light of the sun and the heat of the atmosphere met and gave warmth to the worlds. This brought life.

The ECK entered into the worlds of time and space and began to plant the cosmic eggs of life forms.

Then the SUGMAD moved the gases within the bodies of the worlds and raised the lands above the waters. Life came forth in the waters when the sunlight penetrated the mud, stirring the cosmic eggs planted by the ECK, and life forms appeared.

Again, the sunlight penetrated the dust of the lands, stirring the cosmic eggs planted by the ECK, and from these cosmic eggs life forms came forth.

These life forms were many, and they roamed over the lands and in the seas for yugas upon yugas. Then the SUGMAD looked again and saw that another embodiment was needed to complete the link of the life chain from mineral form to Spirit form. So IT commanded that the apex of life come into embodiment, fashioned after the great Sat Nam, who is the first manifestation of the supreme Deity, and endowed him with power to rule the worlds below the heavens.

Then the spiritual workers created man and placed within him a living imperishable Spirit, called Soul; and man became like the living gods of the spirit worlds with intellectual powers, physical strength, and Soul. He roamed the worlds, living off the creatures of the fields, the fruits of the trees, and the products of the soil.

The mighty SUGMAD spoke to ITS spirits and angels. "Lo, all those who have played in the fields of Heaven shall descend to Earth and take the body form. Each will be given an adi-karma by the Lords of Karma, to carry during his earthly lives. Each shall go through body upon body, reincarnation after reincarnation, until the day comes when he shall meet with me again in the body form in which I shall be known as the Mahanta. Only when he is ready and has reached perfection, when all dross has burned away and he has gained spiritual maturity, will he return to the heavenly fields and become a worker in the spiritual realms. Until then he shall spend his time as Soul, in the lower worlds, learning his catechism and being educated to his true purpose in his heavenly home.

"Each Soul that is created shall go through the fires of the worlds below and be drowned in the seas of tears, agony, and unhappiness, until he cries out for me to reach down to him. Until he has been purified, until he has gone through all the mystic rituals, through the cave of fire and the seas of agony which give him perfection, shall my face be turned from him."

The imperishable spirits called Souls fell upon their knees and wailed their anguish to the heavens. The SUGMAD had spoken and commanded that they go down into the depths of fire, mud, and terror to receive their discipline, to become a Co-worker with the Almighty. Life in eternity had been one of pleasure, play, and happiness, that no mortal being had ever known. To exchange that for a life of misery, unhappiness, and the burdens of karma was more than each Soul could bear.

The SUGMAD closed ITS eyes and dreamed again. The wailing of the Souls did not reach IT. The dreams that came were of creation that formed over the worlds below. IT created, and out of the creation came a manifestation of ITSELF, that mighty Deity whom all mankind knows as the Sat Nam. So mighty is He that few who approach can but believe that here is the Almighty, the Lord of Lords.

The floor of Heaven opened and all Souls went tumbling downward through the worlds, through the planes and regions of light, darkness, the sounds of the wild winds, the universes and heavens. At last, each came to rest upon the worlds of matter—some in the newly formed planets of Venus, Saturn, Jupiter, and those named by man from his little world of Earth. Many came to the Earth planet and formed the consciousness of man in the flesh temple of the human body, to wear the cloth of misery, and unhappiness, and take up the burdens of karma until at last, one day, each would be ready to return to the heavenly home.

Some accepted a human body, others came into consciousness as stone, rocks, minerals, birds, animals, and fish. But all manifestations of the SUGMAD received the consciousness of the lower worlds.

Then there were the rulers of the four planes which were established in the worlds of time and space. First, the SUGMAD manifested ITSELF in the last heavenly plane in ITS own form, which became Sat Nam, the ruler over all worlds in the lower universe.

Under him was formed the spiritual hierarchy of Sohang, Omkar, Ramchar, Jot Niranjan, and Elam, each in order down to the last material plane of the lower universe. At the top of these material worlds the Prince of Darkness took his place to act as the tempter of Soul. He was given the name of Kal Niranjan.

Niranjan is the false power that symbolizes the negative. It is evil, the force that makes Soul believe that happiness lies in material life. It is the Satan of the psychic worlds. All that are tempted by, and succumb to, its whispers of joy and riches shall remain in the fires of torture on the Wheel of Awagawan, or coming and going. This is the age-long cycle of births and deaths, transmigration, the reincarnation of Soul.

Niranjan is the power of mind. It is the psychic power, and those who live in ignorance listen to its sweet whispers of hope. It appeals to the vanity of human consciousness. But it can never succeed, for the Souls who have been pitched into the darkness of the universes shall someday give up and return to their heavenly home to be with the SUGMAD. There they will become workers in the spiritual field somewhere in the worlds of light and love.

Those Souls which follow the beckoning finger of Niranjan to organized religion shall take the wrong turn of the road. None but the Living ECK Master, who has descended to the worlds of matter to give all Souls an opportunity to return to Heaven, is capable of offering this opportunity. All others are false prophets and shall not be heeded.

Those who listen to Niranjan are listening to the false prophet. The sweet whispers of this negative genius are heard in the voices of those who make claims to be the prophets of the times and the preachers, clergy, and priests who represent the old orthodox religions.

Beware, lest they sway you to listen and change toward the Kal Niranjan, who rules the planets of the lower universes. Never talk of achievements in ECK, for this brings only disaster to the chela. Speak not of any achievement nor any loss, for it only brings about the retardation of spiritual attainment.

This is the way of the Kal. Its duty is to arrest the spiritual unfoldment of Soul, and the duty of Soul is to ward off these attempts of Kal.

The human consciousness is prey to autointoxication, for the Kal floods the consciousness of man with various poisons bred by various states of mind and emotion. The most poisonous of these states are fear, anger, worry, sentimental emotionalism, and envy. The destructive emanations set up by these mental emotional states clog the virility and sensitivity of the human race like a heavy pall. The emanations from terrified, slaughtered creatures add to the general aggravation of Kal's works with the human consciousness.

Truth can be understood only by one who is in a state of vigilance; therefore, none who are in a slack condition of mind will find it available. Truth is not in the heights but at the bottom of all things. It must be struggled for and sought after and come upon through earnest effort, through the stimulation brought about by suffering or striving, whereby the consciousness is prepared to recognize it. Truth always appears to be veiled, guarded, and hidden from the eyes of the profane.

At first Souls found little within the worlds of space. There are no boundaries where all is infinite, nor age where time is the only measure of change within the changeless, nor death where life is the indestructible pulse of energy in the heat and the cold. There is no morning, noon, nor evening, for what has always been and will always be, is just what it is.

As there was no beginning for every Soul who came into Its own recognition, there could be no end. But each found in living within the worlds of matter, energy, space, and time, that there is, and has been and always will be, continuous change in the appearance of things which, in the small chronology of finite perceptions, is the life of the human body known as birth and growth, evolution and progress, age and death.

Within the physical universe there occurred in countless eons a stupendous explosion that rearranged the destinies of the suns. One of these smaller suns, a white-hot incandescent splinter of the main sun, fell into the darkness, leaving behind vast streamers. Now shot too far out to return to its parent light, it formed a scattered field of light which came together in irregular orbits around the star it had left. Thus, the world of planets and its neighboring stars were born.

Smaller fires also, thrown far beyond the sun and close to the worlds, held in suspension by the pull of the two, moved over paths of their own. These millions of smaller fires were the scattered fragments of a new solar system, most of them useless. After cooling, after becoming small wandering nuggets of iron and stone, most of these fragments would in time go back to the sun or back to the world of solid matter, the earth.

The universe was not born in a moment nor a million years. It evolved through the ages from the white-hot sparks of the sun to the cold stone enveloping the furnace within its core. Then came the immutable laws to govern the worlds of the universe and bring harmony to the course of those planets that revolved around the hot sun.

Elements became precious within the soils of the Earth and other planets. Out of the heart of the world poured the energies and rhythms and harmonies which were the only substances of God, and the only substance of all things that are.

Like its brother planets, the Earth became a world of its own—a living world, but a simple one of elements where the energies and rhythms were greater than those which were to come in the form of bodies of animals and men. The world made numerous journeys around the sun, a hundred million times or more. Its gaseous body became a liquid and the surface roughly divided into hemispheres and poles. There was no haste, for within the laws of the SUGMAD it was only preparing for the coming of a more complex shape of life.

Thus it became a new world where birth, youth, middle age, old age, and death denoted changes in the appearance of things. The energy of the living God shaped the forms which made the world a cradle of life, the home of civilization, and the graveyard of all embodiments. But never once did it keep the Souls of ITS embodiments within this sphere of the universes.

The SUGMAD destroyed nothing and lost nothing in the process of change. IT only used the world to refine each Soul that entered into IT. IT made the earth a place for greater destiny, through the energies of the ECK flowing down from the Ocean of Love and Mercy.

The long pilgrimage out of the darkness and into the light began in the mud and the slime, working upward

49

into the apex of human consciousness. Something was gained from the cycles of sensate things through birth, age, and sleep, and into life again: They were born higher on the ladder of spiritual consciousness.

The sea was the cradle of life. The magic of the ECK energies formed the complex union of molecules and built a cell of life. The tenacious hold on life of the molecule for existence caused it to wed with others and make a complex entity with tendencies of reaction and response to its environment, the power to move in the water and seek food and protection.

The masses of molecules developed into protozoa and finally into the vegetation of the sea, and, after millions of years, into plants, sponges, and flowers of the watery depths. Minerals developed in the same form on the land surfaces, but the first form that started evolving toward human embodiment was the fish. The Law of ECK moved again in Its very mysterious way and saw the need of organs and faculties in these creatures. Some became aggressive, feeding upon those which had only the vegetation and plants of the sea for survival.

Intelligence came to the creatures of the sea. Simple as it was, it gave those without protection the only means of escape from the devouring jaws of the beasts that swallowed unwary fish. The size and speed of these scourges of the sea grew, developing appetites without parallel. They became sires of the shark, whale, and other mammoth monsters of the deep.

Some of these strange creatures came out of the sea to find easier prey. For a million years this saga went on, with the sea-born and the sea-living moving from the water to the land. Creatures with gills and paddles developed lungs and legs in time. Many walked on hind feet, rearing in the air with crocodile heads and gleaming teeth. Into the dark, dank jungles they went, searching

50

for food. They became stupendous bone-plated machines controlled only by a few lower reflexes, finding beetles as large as sparrows, and flying insects with a wingspread of thirty inches, for their hunger. Anything that walked, crawled, and flew was food for their greed.

These were ancestors of the reptiles. They grew twenty feet in height and fifty feet around. The tail was massive and the skull as large as a grown ox, with broad powerful teeth six inches long. The claws on the feet were curved a little longer than the teeth.

The other species of brutes were just as fearful and frightening of aspect. They seldom attacked one another because of the thick armored skin. Some were vegetarian and others flesh eaters. They were moved by voracious hunger and fear. They were torpid mountains of bone and meat with the sluggish and cold-blooded nervous system of the reptile.

For millions of years these monsters ruled the earth. A few of them became the dragon species that lived on the ground. But smaller dragons took to the air, flying on wings. These were more dreadful than those that walked on the ground.

The ECK's experiment in dreadful creatures came to a sudden and dramatic ending. The dragons that had ruled for millions of years perished within a few centuries, unable to adapt to climatic changes. Too sluggish to migrate and having too little intelligence to understand the coming danger, they froze to death when the great ice age took place.

The ECK was now ready for another kind of creature for experiment and for the first time turned to those to whom It had given sympathy and care. These were the creatures of fear who had lived in dread from the day of birth to the day of death. The destruction of the killer beasts came about in a harsh world, so now the ECK

51

prepared the earth for a more noble experiment for the SUGMAD, the coming of Souls into this world.

The ECK softened and beautified the great, formidable earth, covering the mountains with forests and scatterings of wild flowers over the hills. The valley teemed with butterflies and singing birds. Lights and shadows were given to the morning and evening of the day. Now the mammals entered into the world and became the forerunners of this genus, including man, today.

These were the milk-givers that housed the unborn in their bodies, not by eggs as their fierce predecessors had done. They gave their young care after birth, for now love had entered into the world. The age prior to this was one of tremendous savagery, for often the dragons and other beasts ate their young hatched from eggs, or one another.

However, this was not a gentle age by any means, for still there were the savage beasts, such as the cat family, the saber-tooth tiger and all its kin, the bear, dog, and wolf. There were giant hogs and mammoths, flesh-eaters all of them.

There were two great clans: the killers, who ate only flesh and who spent all their waking hours stalking and killing their prey, and the timid beasts that fed off the earth. Out of these clans came men, who originally were leaf eaters and lived in terror of the killer beasts that stalked and trapped them.

Souls that came into this lower environment had to take on the embodiment of flesh in order to exist in the vibrations of this materialistic world. But man had no place to live for he was prey to the brutality of the flesh eaters. He was not a creature with fangs, claws, and muscular strength. What strength he had was not enough.

He could not venture into the waters for there the beasts awaited ready to tear him apart. In the jungles were the huge serpents and deadly insects; on the prairies were

52

the wolves. There was no spot on earth for him to safely lay his head. He had only one place to live and that was in the trees.

So it was in the high treetops of the forest that he built his home to be safe from the prowling animals that killed him for food. Not the primate, but the Soul and form of man himself. He developed an amazing agility to swing through the higher branches. For ages he was a treetop tenant, rarely venturing to the ground. He drank water from the leaves and ate the foliage, and made his bed in a tree crotch. He scorned the endless spectacle of slaughter which went on beneath him. But the day came when he was to descend to the soil of earth and leave his distant cousins still in the treetops.

At first he walked on four feet, then learned to stand upright, and what was a creature now became a man because he could think, and by thinking he could protect himself. Thereupon, he found a persistent pattern of behavior that set him free. Never again could his supremacy be threatened nor his foe be more than his slave, for they were the beasts of the forest, the birds of the air, and the creatures of the sea.

Then human consciousness came into being, and man became the supreme creature upon the earth.

He developed thought and the ability to use it to protect himself against the flesh killers and the environment. He found shelter in the caves and fashioned weapons out of sticks and stones. He found that the female reproduced his species and he lived in family groups. At first the female was taken by force, for man was a strange and violent creature belonging to the blood-stained and bestial past of the human race. A headman or chief was selected to supervise the family, and the tribe which gathered around him.

Civilization formed in a primitive manner and there

appeared in the world the first ECK Master, who was without name. He was important to the human race because his task was to minister to their needs and give to all succor and wisdom.

Primitive man believed that stones and trees were homes of the spirits who served under supernatural beings who ruled everything. Soul was not yet developed in man for It to understand and know what It was seeking. But It lived in a universe where the laws of the world are different.

Sundered from all things by gulfs and far dimensions, the ancient world of Polara, the Garden of Eden, loomed upon the horizon. Stretching from the greater sea in the east to that in the west, his civilization was known for its great forested lands to the north, the steppes-dwelling creatures, and the fierce desert of the rich eastern lands.

This was the beginning of the races of man upon Earth. Within the world of the past and before the dawn of recorded history, at the western extremity of the continent of Europe, Asia, and Africa, the Polarian, or the Adamic, race of pale copper-skinned people dwelled. Out of the forests came man, walking upright. His first act of worship was for the luminous power that scattered darkness and evil. It was a great golden eye, like a wheel, or a halo of glory, rising majestically out of the underworld with the heat of its body spreading over the whole hungry earth.

The first Polarian man was Adom the Rabi, and he stood on the summit of a hill. His female companion, Ede, stood back with bowed head as he addressed his Sun-god. He prayed for food, protection from pain and enemies, and well-being for his woman.

He was granted everything but freedom from pain and emotion. He knew when the danger came, for out of the forests came another creature walking upright like himself, who wanted the female. The battle was bitter but Adom won and drove off his foe. He produced a man-child and another; and human history began.

Gradually the creatures gathered and formed a clan. Slowly they hacked out the forests, fought the flesh eaters and won, until a civilization was born on the edge of the rivers that flow through the continent called Asia.

Malati, the first ECK Master of record, was sent by the SUGMAD into this world to give man his first spiritual knowledge of God.

For men drifted apart, fought one another for domination over tilled lands, trade, women and slaves, and what little wealth they had in precious stones. Slowly the ECK was building Its species. Then came the race of men called the Hyperboreans, and this became the age of the same name, the second root race of mankind.

The Hyperboreans were the clans that drifted onto land where there was perpetual sunshine. The rains fell heavily upon the forests and created the jungle growth. The north wind never touched the heart of this world and the face of man became darkened by the sun and jungle regions.

Where the Polarian man was a tiller of the soil, a shepherd and a hunter, his successor was a higher being who built cities and founded a civilization in the heart of the equatorial jungle. He developed weapons for fighting, and pots for holding his food. He elected a king to rule over the mighty empire of Melnibora.

The empire lived on for a hundred centuries, ruled over by the fierce Varkas kings. They swept across the jungles and over the heat of the sands to the north, conquering the wild tribes of men with white skins.

They made slaves of the conquered, forcing them to work in their fields, in their weapons shops, and in the homes of their nobility. The kings ruled by the formless

55

terror called sorcery, with powers greater than anything witnessed prior to their times and for centuries to come.

The Varkas used their awful powers to conquer their subjects and their foes. They cast spells upon the masses and dealt in terrible mysteries with the dead. Some of the kings conquered time and lived for centuries. They ruled through the priests who were known as the Zuajirs. And these priests were more terrible than their masters.

They were ruthless, giving quarter to no man when captured on the field of battle. The victim was killed or saved for a fate more fearful than anything man could believe. If he was saved for the stables of the nobleman or to work in some household, the captured was indeed fortunate.

Living in secret and teaching to those who would give ears was the great Kai-Kuas, the Living ECK Master of these times. He was discovered by the Varkas and slain.

This was an age when man literally ate man, for he was hardly out of the jungle and felt that all life was his deadly enemy. He believed that in order to survive, he must serve his god, the sun, and when night fell, it was the destruction of their god. When it rose again in the morning, its worshipers knew the sun had won over the powers of darkness and evil.

Along with this, it was their simple belief that the people of the north with their pale skins were evil and, therefore, must be subjected. They conquered and ruled the world as the first of the races to go out trying to subject its fellowmen by the sword.

Soon they began to lose their hold on the known world, for the ECK experimented with Its own species and founded a third root race known as the Lemurians. This new race, living in the land of Lemuria, was brown skinned with a highly developed sense toward being civilized.

The Lemurians had the greatest civilization known to the world. It developed on the great continent of Mu in the midst of the western ocean, and spread around the world with many subempires. It was a tropical country of vast plains. The valleys and plains were covered with rich grazing grass and tilled fields. There were only low rolling hills and no mountains, for the peaks and ranges of great heights had not yet been forced up from the deep centers of the earth.

The air was soft, the vegetation constantly bloomed, and life for the millions of the continent's people was gay and happy. Ten tribes made up the bulk of the citizens, each distinct but living under an emperor named Ra Mu. The empire was named the "Empire of the Sun."

Ra Mu was the representative of the Supreme Deity, although he was not worshiped. The deity was worshiped through symbols, and all believed in the immortality of Soul, which eventually returned to the Source from whence It came.

The reverence of the Lemurians for their deity was so great they never spoke Its name and even in prayer and supplication addressed It always through a symbol. However, Ra, the sun, was used as the collective for all that the deity possessed as a supreme entity.

The people of Mu were highly civilized and enlightened. They were gentle, peaceful, and lived together without savagery. As citizens of the great empire which stretched from rising sun to rising sun—an empire upon which the sun never set—they were under the protection of Mu, the motherland of the earth.

The ruling race of Mu was exceedingly handsome, with brown or olive skin, large, soft, dark eyes and straight black hair. They had other races—the yellow, brown, and black people—but these did not dominate. They sailed

57

the seas and discovered new lands, inhabited and established colonies around the globe, built great temples, stone palaces, and carved gigantic monuments.

Within the continent of Mu were seven major cities, where the religion, science, and education centers existed. There also were many other large cities for trading and industry, for, as the center of the world as it came to be known, Mu was the land where all came for learning, trading, and commerce. The rest of the world formed her colonies.

Into this world came Geutan, the third great ECK Master, who served the people of Mu and warned them of the coming destruction of the world.

When this continent was at its zenith, the center of world civilization, it received a terrible shock.

The rumblings from the bowels of the earth, followed by earthquakes and volcanic outbursts, shook her southern parts. Gigantic, cataclysmic waves from the ocean rolled over the land and the cities went down to destruction. The volcanoes belched out their fire, smoke, and lava. The flat continent reared up and lava beds formed cones which became rocks.

After this, the people of Mu gradually overcame their fright; cities were rebuilt, and trade and commerce were resumed. Generations passed after this visitation, and when the phenomenon had become history, Mu again became the victim of earthquakes. The whole continent heaved and rolled like ocean waves. The land trembled and shook like leaves on a tree in a storm. Temples and palaces came crashing to the ground and monuments and statues were overturned. The cities became heaps of ruins.

The land quivered and shook, rose and fell. The fires of the earth underneath flamed forth and pierced the clouds. Thick black palls of smoke hung over the land

and huge cataclysmic waves rolled through the cities and plains. The terrified people sought refuge in their temples and citadels only to be driven out by the fire and smoke.

During the night the land was torn apart, and down it went into the dark waters of the ocean, claiming the lives of millions of people. The waves rolled over and met in the center of the land, seethed and boiled, destroying the Earth's first great civilization.

A few islands were left where mountain peaks had been raised in the catastrophe. Those people who survived this terrible event became the race of the South Sea Islands.

From across the world there came next into existence the Atlantean race, the fourth root race, or the red race, who lived upon the continent of Atlantis in the great ocean between the eastern and western hemispheres. It grew steadily with large cities and fair lands, with tilled fields and deep valleys. The people worshiped the supreme deity they called Tat, who represented the four corners of the world; East, West, North and South.

Atlantis replaced Mu as the center of the world and became the greatest civilization of its time with learning, trade, and commerce. It had over a hundred million people living on its lands. But this world was rife with magic, and its king-priests, called the Tat Tsoks, were wizards of cruelty who ruled over all with an iron hand.

Castrog, the Living ECK Master, came into this world to teach these olive-skinned people that the Supreme Deity was not happy with their ways and dealings in black magic. He suffered the death of the sword for his troubles, but not before warning the king that his lands and people would soon die under the waters of the sea.

One generation later the catastrophe which had sunk the land of Mu brought death to all the fourth root race, leaving only a dark, unsmiling ocean to greet the sailors who dared to cross its surface.

The fifth root race, the Aryans, developed the magnificent empire of Uighur in central Asia in the Gobi Desert. It was a mighty land stretching from the Pacific Ocean across central Asia and eastern Europe. The history of this empire is the history of the Aryan race. Its capital city was in the Gobi Desert, then a fertile land and large in the sense that it was the center of the world in its day, with a highly developed civilization.

The Living ECK Master, Rama, first known to the civilized world of the Aryans, came out of the high valleys of Tibet to the capital city of Khara Khota and began preaching ECKANKAR. But he was hounded out of the empire and went back into Tibet, where he founded the monastery of Katsupari in the northern mountains.

From there he went into India to teach the great science of ECKANKAR to its teeming masses.

The sixth root race is the yellow race, coming on the heels of the gradually fading Aryan race. It is the Mongoloid race of the East, which has its life center in the world of the North, where many do not penetrate. The ECK Master who will come into this world of semidarkness and light will be Regnard. This race is yet to fulfill its destiny on the Earth planet. It will meet destruction by fire, earthquakes, and tidal waves.

The seventh root race will be the golden race, and they will be called the Zohar people. They will come from a far distant planet to colonize the world after its destruction by another great catastrophe in the twenty-first and twenty-second centuries. The attempt to put colonies on this planet will fail and eventually, after several centuries, these peoples will withdraw.

The ECK Master who will be responsible for the spiritual welfare of this race will be Sepher.

The SUGMAD will then withdraw all Souls from all planets and constellations into the heavenly worlds where they will sleep until IT has repaired the damage to the lower world planets. Those who have to return will then be sent back again to finish their spiritual development in this world.

4

The Kingdom of the SUGMAD

The great doctrine of liberation taught by the Mahanta is set forth here for all who have earned the right to know. If he has the ears to hear and the eyes to see, all knowledge and glory will be given unto him.

Every Soul is liberated from the material worlds upon initiation by the Mahanta, who has been granted this power by the SUGMAD. As the representative of the Supreme Deity in all planes below the Anami Lok, he in turn releases and transfers the consciousness of spiritual freedom to all who desire to have freedom through the ECK.

Release comes at the time of initiation, not at the transference of Soul from the physical body at death in the material plane. Those who become the initiates of the Inner Circle of ECK live out their lives in the physical plane, and are transported at the time of death into the higher worlds without standing in the court of Yama, the King of the Dead, where all uninitiated Souls must go to receive judgment for their earthly actions.

The uninitiated are those who have not received liberation through initiation from the Mahanta. Baptism will not fulfill the necessity of liberation. Neither will the joining of any cult, religion, or faith. Only the Living ECK Master has the power to initiate Souls and take them to the regions of light.

The initiated Soul is transported from the temple of flesh at the time of death by the Mahanta, to confront the clear light of the Atma Lok. It has left behind the body and will never return to embodiment on this earthly planet. It is now free and will take up Its assignments in the Kingdom of the SUGMAD for eternity.

Faith is the first step on the secret pathway to heaven. Unless the chela believes in the Mahanta, has faith in the ECK, and trusts the SUGMAD—completely—he has spent his time worthlessly.

The faith that one has in the Mahanta must be that of complete understanding and surrender. Whatever the Mahanta sees, knows, and understands about the ECK chela is his own secret. He never tells but expects the chela to give a degree of obedience and observance to his desires, all of which are for the benefit of the chela. He never expects anything less than self-surrender of the chela to the divine will that is working through him as the Inner Master.

Those who cease to believe in the Mahanta must pay the price. The payment is in accord with their degree of capability. Since the Inner Master is only the vehicle for the SUGMAD, all persons who are following the path of ECK must look to him as the representative of the ECK power on earth.

He is not the Master of anyone who is not following the path of ECKANKAR. He is the Avatar, the Master, the guide and vehicle of the Divine Being for anyone who is immersed in the spiritual works of ECK.

The Mahanta takes over the spiritual life of whomever approaches him to become a chela. He guides him through his worldly life and helps him to resolve all his karma here before being translated into the other worlds. Upon entering these worlds permanently, the chela finds the Master still guiding him spiritually. At no time does the Mahanta ever leave one who has become his charge, regardless of whether or not the chela tries to break his ties. The tie is never broken inwardly—perhaps outwardly, but never on the inner planes.

The ECK Master establishes miraculous power in the chela when they meet for the chela's last incarnation in this earth world. Thus when the chela is ready, when he has reached that stage of spiritual development, a meeting with the Living ECK Master is inevitable.

When any man or woman has earned the right to stand before the Mahanta, there is no power in the universe that can keep him away from the Sat Guru. The two must meet, for the spiritual law commands it. But in every case it is good karma that brings the individual to the Mahanta. The proof is in itself, for when the chela is ready the Mahanta will find him.

The Mahanta is prepared to take the chela into the heavenly worlds of the SUGMAD. These worlds are the Atma Lok, Alakh Lok, Alaya Lok, Hukikat Lok, Agam Lok, and the Anami Lok. It is above the Anami Lok where dwells the Lord of Lords. This is also the true home of the Atma, that particle of God which has been sent down into the lower worlds to receive purification.

These are the pure worlds of the SUGMAD. It is the universe of the ECK, where there is neither time, space, matter, nor motion. It is where all karma and reincarnation have ended, and the Atma is a part of the whole, but individual in Itself. It is here that the Atma receives, by choice, Its mission in the lower worlds to become a Co-worker with God.

The bodies of man within the lower worlds assume the

embodiment of sex, either male or female. Thereby, reproduction in the lower worlds, especially in the material universes, is accomplished through sex. But within the heavenly world of the Anami Lok, Souls are reproduced by the Lord of Lords reacting upon ITSELF. Therefore, every Soul is a particle of the divine Source which is known as the Supreme Being. Each is a spark of the Divine Self.

The Atma—Soul—is a neuter atom of the Divine Source of life. It is neither male nor female, masculine nor feminine, man nor woman. It is both within the worlds of God. It does not assume a body until reaching the worlds below the Atma Plane, the fifth plane.

Thereupon It takes a body of either sex in the beginning, usually that of the male during Its first incarnation. Following this, It will take the body of the female; thereafter, during Its millions of incarnations in the physical worlds, Soul will alternate between male and female bodies, each time learning some lessons while gathering karma and working off karma.

The good karma will be kept while the negative karma will be given up as the burden of learning the lessons of life. The final goal of good karma is to bring the chela to the Living ECK Master and to learn the true path to the SUGMAD. This is the very highest reward of good karma, assuring the chela of his liberation from the Wheel of the Eighty-Four.

The true works of ECKANKAR take the chela into the heavenly world to become a Co-worker with God. There is nothing higher than this. When the chela asks what his mission is in life, he should be told that becoming a Co-worker with God is the only purpose of Soul's existence.

He begins his true spiritual life in the Atma Plane which is known to all as the Soul world. The classical name for this plane is the Sat Nam, who also is the ruler of this world. This is the first realm of the SUGMAD, the pure Being, where Soul finds Self-Realization. It is the dividing plane between the worlds of pure Spirit and those of the negative worlds. The Sound here is the single note of a flute. The chant one gives is the name of the Divine Being, the SUGMAD!

The next plane is the Alakh Lok, known as the invisible plane. Its classical name is the same, and the chanting here is *Shanti*. In the Hindu language it means *peace*. This is the second world of the SUGMAD. It is ruled by the great being Alakh Purusha, who at times seems harsh and without consideration, although the chanting in this world does not seem to fit the nature of its ruler. The sound of the ECK here is the wind, sometimes roaring and sometimes very gently sighing, like a breeze in the treetops.

The Alaya Lok is the third pure spiritual plane above the Atma region. It is the true shining world, sometimes called the Sach Khand. The chanting here is a sort of hum, like that done with the lips closed tightly and humming a worldly tune. The description here is of endless worlds for it is so vast, so far beyond any conception of man's intelligence. The ruler of this plane is the Alaya Purusha, a mighty being whose very presence fills every Soul with awe as he passes through this world.

The Hukikat Lok is the fourth world which Soul must travel through on Its way to the SUGMAD, the center of all universes. This is the highest state that Soul usually reaches. It is the plane of God-Realization where Soul learns the God-knowledge. The Sound is like the music of a thousand violins. The chanting is the word *Aluk*. The great being here is the Huki Purusha, the Lord of the fourth world of pure Spirit.

The Agam Lok is the fifth world, the inaccessible plane.

Few Souls go past the Hukikat Lok into this world. It is a world of immense space, so much greater than any which the mind could ever conceive. The Sound here is delicate music, something that cannot be described. It is like the music of woodwinds—faint, sweet, and beautiful. A melody that gives Soul great ecstasy. The word here is *Huka*, and it is pronounced HU-KA. The lord of this world is the Agam Purusha and he is the guardian of the Anami Lok, the nameless plane.

The Anami Lok is the world of the Supreme Being, the SUGMAD. This is the Lord of Lords, the highest of all Beings, and ITS home is the Ocean of Love and Mercy. IT does not live in a palace nor dwell on a throne, as many believe. ITS home is the mighty center of the universes, the very heart and core of all life and existence. IT dwells in the center of this mammoth ocean where all is like a whirlpool, sending out ITS Word to the worlds upon worlds.

The Word, the Voice of the SUGMAD, goes forth like a wave from the center of a pond and sings Its way through all the planes in many different songs and melodies. Each is the living Word, creating and giving life to everything in each world. By Its very life—this ECK, the essence of the SUGMAD, the Spirit of all things—life exists.

When It reaches the end of the worlds It returns like the wave, gathering up all Souls that are ready to do God's work. They are returned to the true home and become Co-workers with God, having completed their mission in life.

The true gospel of ECK is to give every chela Truth. This truth is to lift him into the worlds of Light and Sound; the Kingdom of the SUGMAD. Thereby the spiritual law of God acts upon the fact that it is possible for every Soul to unfold spiritually, in a greater or lesser degree, in one direction or another. He may seek to order his life and his relations with the SUGMAD on the basis of the knowledge that he must become a Co-worker with the Divine Being.

The chela must practice *Pratyahara,* the complete withdrawal of consciousness from the environment around himself. This is true on every plane of the universe below the Atma world. The chela cannot fail to do otherwise or he will delay his ascendance into the heavenly Kingdom of God. He shall delay his true mission, which is to serve out his spiritual responsibilities in a world of heavenly good.

Heaven is the ultimate state. It is where Soul goes to meet Its Maker and decide upon Its final mission in eternity. Soul alone must make the choice of what It shall do for Its missionary assignment. This is the freedom of choice which the SUGMAD gives to all Souls. No other form of life has this privilege.

Soul sometimes enters this universe as a thing of lower embodiment. Generally, It enters into the minerals of the earth, where It will dwell for an age. In succession It becomes the flower, the fish, a denizen of the seas and waters of the lands, a serpent, a creature of the air, the treetop things, a four-legged animal, and after many such incarnations It enters into the body of man.

Man lives only with himself. He is the ablest of all the creatures of God, for the use of the divine power of ECK is at his fingertips. He learns to use this and to liberate himself from the Kal power which rules the lower universes. But it is only with the spiritual assistance of the Mahanta that he is able to do this. The mind, of itself, is of little use to him except to live within the physical plane.

The mind is only an instrument for the Atma to use within this world of matter. It uses the mind and the physical and mental facilities like one uses a machine. Man is only an animal without the Atma. He is the physical body known to all in the spiritual works of ECK as the *Isthul Sharir.* Unless the chela denies the existence of matter this cannot be disputed. It gets hurt, sick, and dies to return to the soil from which it originally came.

Within the Physical body is that starry and subtle body, the *Sukhsham Sharir* or Nuri Sarup, the light body of the Astral world. It sparkles with millions of particles like stars shining in the worldly heavens. It is through this body that the mind and Soul can communicate with the Physical body and its world. But it will take shape according to the character of the individual. Therefore, the chela knows what his Astral body is according to his natal ECK-Vidya-scope. When the Physical body dies this Nuri Sarup stays as the instrument of expression on the Astral plane.

Within the Astral body is another body, more subtle and much lighter, which is called the *Karan Sharir.* This is the Causal body, which is quite distinct from the Astral. It is named this because it is the real cause, containing the seeds of all that is ever to take place in the individual's life. This is the body that the Living ECK Master reads for the past, present, and future of the individual.

The other body enclosed within the Causal body is the Manas, or Mental Sharir. It is much more refined than the other two bodies. It would appear to the eye as a blue globe of light and has a humming sound when in the presence of another. Its function is to act as a transformer for thought between the mind and the astral body. It is creative to an extent, but only because it receives impressions from the *Buddhi Sharir,* which is known as the Etheric, or subconscious, mind.

The Buddhi Sharir lies between the Mental body and Soul. It is regarded as the part of the mind body which acts as a sheath between mind and Soul: It is very

70

sensitive to impressions from Soul, and its function is to receive and transmit impressions between mind and Soul on the one side, and between Soul and mind on the other. A perfect record of every experience the individual has ever had in any incarnation within the countless ages of Its existence throughout any plane is stored here. These can be read by the Living ECK Master by use of the ECK-Vidya.

The Atma Sarup is the Soul body. It is the Atma Sharir which dwells on the Fifth Plane, the dividing line between the material worlds and the true spiritual regions. It is a broad, universal world that takes in the whole of all things, including the lower and the higher universes. It is an extremely sensitive body and is, in Its natural state, a perfect vessel of the Divine Being. Only by Its compulsive lives in the bodies of the lower worlds does It appear to become imperfect. It becomes covered with a sheath, making It seem imperfect, but this is only the illusion of the Kal forces.

Spiritual liberation comes when one finds himself established in the Atma Sarup. The recognition of enlightenment within the state of Soul Consciousness brings Light and Sound at this particular plane which is a blazing illumination similar to the light of ten thousand suns. The roaring is more thunderous than that of ten thousand waterfalls.

It is here that Soul enters into Self-Realization. It finds Itself in the state of Self Awareness. The universal mission of being a Co-worker with the SUGMAD is rapidly realized in Soul's state of self-knowledge. It knows and now is ready to advance into the heavenly worlds of true Spirit. It has no other purpose in life and all attachments to the life in the lower worlds are lost. The values of materialistic things leave the senses of the mind and body, for now Soul is in control of all life around Itself.

All Souls must, in the beginning of their creation, descend into the bowels of Turiya Pad. This is where the SUGMAD declared they must dwell until each becomes once more fitted to serve IT and not the pleasures of desire.

The highest form of belief is faith-belief in the SUGMAD. The higher always encompasses the perfection of the lower. To act as if we are. This is the secret of believing, of having faith in the SUGMAD. "Believing is not believing," so says the Lord of Lords to all Souls who descend into the ash can of the universes.

"I say unto you, believe in my Word. For the day shall come when you shall doubt all things. The earth shall be rocked in its last convulsion, and when ye have spent life after life seeking and finding nothing, then ye shall offer up everything to me, begging for the life which is already yours for the faith in me!"

And the Lord of Lords spoke again: "To him who will love me and will observe my commandments will I manifest myself; and he shall be one with me and I with him."

Those who love the SUGMAD shall be taken unto ITS heart and given the Kingdom of Heaven. But those who do not love the SUGMAD and wish to go their way shall not have the Kingdom of Heaven nor any of ITS parts.

This must be written on the heart of every Soul for all things and all life are concerned with the Lord of Lords. If the Tuza, or Soul, chooses to forget and gives Its devotion to Kal Niranjan, that Tuza shall become a slave and have only the transitory objects of the lower kingdom, ruled over by the Kal alone.

Soul journeys through the worlds of the Kal. Whenever It finds that it is time to leave the physical vehicle in which It has abided for Its time in this lower world, then a preparation is made to enter into the Astral body, the first of the inner bodies.

72

This Astral body becomes truly awakened with the advent of Soul, for the physical and all states of consciousness are left in the outer body. It dwells in this first inner vehicle for a relative period of time, then either proceeds into the Causal body, or returns to another physical embodiment. This is known as reincarnation.

Soul must leave the physical body at the death of this temple of clay and journey into the next world. This passing is called the *Kangra Sambha*. It is known as the supraspiritual experience of Soul. Thus, it leads to a knowledge of the greater worlds beyond the physical senses. This journey, the Kangra Sambha, takes place between the Physical worlds and the Astral. This is the Bardo of Tibetan Buddhism, the purgatory of the Christians. It is the duty of the Mahanta to assist the Atma when It passes from the physical body and enters into the Kangra Sambha period of Its journey.

After this death of a physical vehicle, the Atma is taken by the Living ECK Master to whatever subtle region of the inner worlds It has earned. No Soul that is an initiate of ECK will have to account for Its deeds and actions within the lower realm of the Kal world. It is through with all earthly karma and must now begin to work out the karma of Its actions on the Astral Plane.

The Physical world is a world of turmoil and strife. Never shall there be any peace in it. This is the way of the SUGMAD. It is so designed that the Pinda worlds shall have nothing but strife, for the good of each Soul that must dwell therein. For these worlds are the testing ground of Soul; the place It must spend Its long periods of existence, creating perfection and spiritual maturity.

Should the Soul not be an initiate of the Living ECK Master, It must stand before Dharam Raya, the Judge of the Kangra Sambha, and receive Its just award. There are no complaints nor favors, and justice is rendered to all.

73

Each Soul knows It is being judged and must consent to the judgment. It is then taken to the region or condition where It has earned Its residence, be it good or bad. It remains there for a fixed time according to the judgment rendered. After Its time has expired, It is then returned to this world, or some other world, to once more begin a new life in the physical body. It takes up where It left off, somewhere in one of Its past lives, and starts once again, depending upon Its karma.

The Kingdom of the SUGMAD is imperishable. Thus, when Soul enters into this region of Light It either remains or is given a mission somewhere in the lower kingdom. But It knows immortality and the joy of serving with the SUGMAD to keep the vast universes running smoothly.

Soul derives benefit from all that the SUGMAD gives It through the grace of the Lord of Lords. It is so far removed from Its true home that without the spiritual benefits of the perfect Sat Guru, the Mahanta, It cannot find Its way back.

All chelas on the path of ECK, though belonging to different historical periods and various times of study under a Living ECK Master during their past lives, have now come to the level in this life to be completely released from all karma, or else to make progress toward resolving that karma so each may be liberated within the near future.

Many, started by the force of their spiritual exercises, have already reached certain levels in their unfoldment. But all of them have not yet reached the final stage. This is why they are still struggling to find the way. Some of them have stopped at the First Plane level and others at the Second. Only the ECK Masters have reached the fifth stage of spiritual development, where they enter into the Atma Plane at will. They have gone far beyond this stage and entered into the Anami level with the true Godhead.

This is the place of the original departure of Soul toward the lower regions. During Its downward journey, Soul goes through such intermediate states as the Agam Lok, Hukikat Lok, Alaya Lok, Alakh Lok, Sat Lok, and the Saguna Lok (the subconscious, or Etheric Plane); Brahm Lok (the Mental Plane); Brahmanda Lok (the Causal Plane); Sat Kanwal-Anda Lok (the Astral Plane); and the Pinda (the Physical Plane).

Once in the Physical worlds the curtain of memory is drawn down over the mind. Here Soul struggles for centuries, through life after life, wondering if the journey through time is worthy of Its efforts. A few will rise into the Astral world and feel that this is the true Kingdom of the SUGMAD. They feel that Soul originated here and has returned home again. This is the illusion of the Kal whose responsibility is the play of the universe, the sport of the gods; to amuse itself at the expense of Soul struggling toward the true Godhead.

The follower of ECKANKAR is never alone for the Mahanta, the Living ECK Master is always with him at the Atma Sarup, or Atma body. The chela may never realize it but, nevertheless, it is true. Once Soul has joined with the ECK Master upon the true path of God, there is never a separation. The chela may wander about for many lives trying to find himself, trying to return to the path, but the Living ECK Master has never left him. He never recognizes this because of the veil of materiality that has covered his eyes.

Each ECKist should practice the Kundun. The Kundun means "the presence" of the Living ECK Master. Whether or not he can see the form of the Master, he must try to hold a conversation through mental whisperings. He should listen for the answers which come via the intuitive or the mental arena. He should never be in doubt that the Master has spoken to him from the inner world.

If the chela practices looking into the Tisra Til—the Spiritual Eye—where the Inner Master, the Mahanta, dwells in every Soul, he will find him there.

The chela first meets the Mahanta in the first region of the Astral worlds. This is the next station above the Tisra Til. It is known as the Ashta-dal-Kanwal, the lotus center of eight petals, located just below the true center of all the Astral worlds, the Sahasra-dal-Kanwal. This is the great city capital of the First Plane beyond the Physical world.

Between the Ashta-dal-Kanwal and the Sahasra-dal-Kanwal lie the Sun Worlds and the Moon Worlds, sometimes called the Lightning Worlds. Here is where the chela who practices the Spiritual Exercises of ECK meets with the Mahanta to travel into the far worlds for Self-Realization; to eventually enter into God-Realization, where he will have the whole of divine wisdom.

The Mahanta is able to be seen by all his chelas simultaneously for he is of the ECK Itself. Being the Spirit of all things he is, therefore, capable of giving the secret teachings to all initiates of ECKANKAR, or to protect and give them all the necessities of life. He knows what goes on in the minds of every chela and all people. If he so chooses he knows the thoughts of animals and of every embodiment of life.

He is the true Master. If the chela practices the Spiritual Exercises of ECK, then at a point between the Sun Worlds and the Moon Worlds he will enter the zone known as the Ashta-dal-Kanwal. It is here that the great change is made which alters his life and his method of procedure. This change is the meeting with the Mahanta, who appears just as he does in the Physical body except his radiant body is more beautiful, and brilliantly illuminated. The Mahanta appears and greets the chela with great joy. From that moment on the two are never separated throughout their lives, whether it is in the physical world or on the spiritual planes. The form of the Mahanta is always with the chela from the moment he enters into the path of ECK, although the chela does not see him as a general rule.

The ECKist must always practice the Kundun, the presence, whether or not he can see this inner body of the Master. It can, however, be noted many times by the outer manifestations of things such as the protection gained, the great feeling of love which surrounds the chela, the improvement of his welfare, and the attainment of spiritual knowledge. All is given freely to the ECKist after he has passed into the higher worlds via Soul Travel.

It has been mentioned that above the Atma Lok (the fifth world) are the high worlds. This is the region of the ECK Masters and there are numerous planes still further above which have not yet been revealed by these Adepts. Out of love for all the struggling masses of humanity, they are now able to bring forth the description of the worlds above and below the Atma Lok.

There are two worlds of the mind, the Brahmandi and the Pindi. But the chela is not concerned with these for they are within the lower worlds and must be used to carry on the business of the world with the help of Soul. Soul becomes so attached to the mind that It is caught in a downward pull toward the lower physical regions. The mind and sense organs receive their power of action from Soul. Once Soul, the Atma, turns toward Its true home in the heavenly worlds of the SUGMAD, all Its attachment to the physical worlds begins to decrease.

When Soul reaches Its home in the Atma Plane beyond the regions of the Brahm, the mind, It is freed from all bonds whether they have been causal, astral, physical, sensual, or mental. Attachment to the world is then only in name and can be terminated at Its own volition.

The rope of the conscious tie with the spiritual self can only be cut when the Atma reaches this place of abode. This is accomplished by Soul freeing Itself from the chains of the mind and senses. The unconscious part of one's life, which is controlled by the Etheric, or subconscious, mind, consists of the mind, senses, vital organs, and the worldly patterns of karma which have been established from past lives and must be cut by the Living ECK Master.

The highest of all the spiritual regions, the Kingdom of the SUGMAD, cannot be described in mortal language. It is the Anami, the nameless region. Sometimes it is called the "untold region." This is the beginning and the ending of all worlds. It is the love and power of this world that vibrates throughout the worlds by the force of the SUGMAD, the first principle.

Five worlds below the Anami, the Kingdom of the SUGMAD, is found the Atma Lok, which is highly effulgent and pure. It is the world of pure Spirit and consciousness. It is the beginning and ending of all creation of the lower worlds. The currents emanate from this plane and spread into all regions below. Sat Nam, the great ruler of this plane, is the true manifestation of the SUGMAD and is the creator of all the worlds below. The ECK flows down from this world manifesting embodiments and the entities who inhabit all the worlds below.

This is the home of the ECK Masters. They are the embodiments or incarnations of the Lord of this region. Love, mercy, and bliss reign here eternally. All those aspects known as death, karma, sin, evil, and pain are not found in this region. This is the first stage of the journey to God in the true spiritual worlds. Until Soul has reached this plane It is still in the clutches of Kal Niranjan in the planes of the Universal Mind Power.

During the present Kali-Yuga age, the dark age, all humanity has become tormented by the thousand ills of poverty, disease, plagues, and wars instigated by jealousy, which remove man from the path of Truth. Seeing that this had happened in the worlds of the lower path, the SUGMAD was moved to incarnate ITSELF as the Mahanta, the Living ECK Master and to give the truth of the path of salvation in simple language.

The agents of Kal, who call themselves men of God, have concealed and done away with all truly religious scriptures. They have replaced them with the pseudo-scriptures, and claim they are the books of God.

The ECK Masters have for centuries explained to the people the mystery of the ECK, the Word, in their own written and spoken language. They have given the words of the golden scripts—the Shariyat-Ki-Sugmad—and initiated disciples into the true teachings of ECKANKAR. Therefore the teachings of the SUGMAD are upon every plane of the universes of universes. Each plane has a portion of this holy manuscript, according to the understanding of the chelas who reach this plane.

Those who watch over and guard the golden scripts of the SUGMAD are the nine unknown Gods of Eternity. They are different from the ECK Masters who act as the teachers, instructors and watch-guards for the portions of the Shariyat-Ki-Sugmad kept upon each plane. The nine unknown Gods are the keepers of the Divine Flame of Wisdom. They let only a few into their temples to learn the deeper knowledge of what the secret truths might hold for them.

Man loves miracles. But a religion based only on miracles or a show of the supernatural powers cannot endure permanently. As long as a doctrine or principle is not fully comprehended by the reasoning faculty in its spiritual aspects, it is not likely to stay with the mind for

79

any length of time.

Many profess faith in ECK outwardly, but have not given up their longing for materiality in their hearts. This lack of faith is due to their ignorance of the spiritual works of ECK. Often they do not take the pains to read or study properly, nor do they listen to the Mahanta. They criticize and harp upon their pains and troubles, often blaming the Living ECK Master, and in their ignorance they do not understand that this is a dangerous practice. Everything they say against the Mahanta and the ECK will return and take from them. Their losses are due to their own thoughts and actions.

The chela who has the society of the Mahanta, the perfect Vi-Guru, will partake of the Grace of God and love. He has started upon the true path to the Kingdom of the SUGMAD. There is a difficulty here, too, for often the Vi-Guru is apt to be regarded as an ordinary man serving his own interests, and the chela may refuse to submit himself wholly to the discipline which the Mahanta asks of him.

The Mahanta does not desire that worldly people in large numbers flock after him. He prefers only those who are eager for the realization of God to them. He does not perform miracles for people to see, but moves in the mysterious ways of the Lord. The true disciple does not believe in the miracles which the Mahanta may perform at varied times but instead believes in the teachings he imparts to give each a lift into the heavenly worlds.

Slander and criticism should strengthen the faith of the chelas for the Mahanta, the Living ECK Master. Only a true devotee can resist the evil effects of malicious opposition. To put up with insult and slander is a mark of true love. None but the true lovers and devotees are able to rise above the fear of censure and the world's disapproval.

The Lord saith that, "Slander or mockery of the followers of ECK is a guard for the market of love and a cleaner of its dirt.

"Only those who love the ECK, and listen only to the music of the heavenly worlds, will enter into the true Kingdom. They will repel the scorn and slander of the world like water falling from the rubber tree leaf when the rain falls from the sky.

"He who believes in me shall be saved. He who scorns my loved ones shall suffer in the fires of the tormented and shall not enter into the heavenly kingdom until he repents of his words and deeds."

5

The Spiritual Hierarchy

Those who follow ECKANKAR are never alone. The presence of the Living ECK Master is always with the ECKist, regardless of wherever he is in the invisible worlds or whatever he is doing in his life.

Fortunate is he who believes in the Living ECK Master, the Mahanta. If he has faith in the Mahanta, in the lords of the other worlds, and the ECK Masters, then he will have good fortune in wealth and health. He will be known to his neighbors as the most fortunate of all men.

If he believes in Kal Niranjan, the king of the Kal (negative) worlds, he will be unfortunate for he will be a slave, a man who suffers and has great hardships. He will have neither money nor health. His faith in the king of the Kal worlds will only bring him misfortune and unhappiness in any world where he may dwell. The face of the Living ECK Master is turned away from him and the spiritual lords of all the worlds know him not.

Only the God-governed shall inherit the worlds. The false belief that there is something besides the SUGMAD and the perfect spiritual creation is thriving in the lower worlds and is responsible for the discord in the human race. This false belief that there is life, substance, and intelligence without the SUGMAD is an illusion which Kal Niranjan wishes for each Soul in the human embodiment to possess.

This false belief is the counterfeit of spiritual reality. It is the illusion of the material senses that sees only the material universe inhabited by physical beings, each with a limited mind of his own embedded in matter.

This erroneous concept gives rise to the idea of faith in something other than the ECK. Belief in anything except the ECK is false and does not alter reality any more than a passing cloud would permanently hide the sunlight. Most chelas, including those who follow the ECK, are too hidden in the matter world, the illusions of the Kal.

All in the lower regions, except the ECK, is controlled by the Kal. When in humility one is able to look away from his wrangling, self-assertive human consciousness—his own and others'—recognizing his true spiritual identity, then he recognizes himself.

The foundation of all is uncreated, uncompounded, independent, and beyond the conception of the human senses and verbal definition. Nothing can describe what this is. Neither the term God, nor the term Anami Lok, can be applied to IT. To realize IT is to attain the Mahanta state. Not to realize IT is to wander in the Kal worlds.

Not knowing the source of all, beings err. They are overwhelmed by the darkness of the unconscious Kal power from which springs ignorance and error. So immersed in error and so obscured by ignorance, the seeker becomes fearful and bewildered. From this state springs the concept of the individual "I," the ego, and the "others."

It is only when these have gained strength and matured in all beings that there is an unbroken current in the evolution of the lower embodiments in the worlds of

Kal. It is here that the five passions of the mind reign. Lust, anger, greed, attachment, and vanity flourish, and they produce an interminable chain of the Kal karma.

Thus, the root source of error among lower beings is unconscious ignorance. It is only through the power of the SUGMAD that each of them is able to realize the radiant innate Self in all living things.

There is a remedy for this ignorance, for the Lord says, "He who asks in my name shall receive all blessings, provided he is worthy."

"But if he is one who gives my message to the world and acts at all times in my name, he shall be among those who are indeed worthy and greatly blessed."

This is the promise of the SUGMAD. If the chela gives in the name of the Living ECK Master, all is blessed and he shall receive. If he gives all in the name of the SUGMAD, the chela is also blessed. Little does the nature of the deed change and he is blessed for he is indeed worthy.

All blessings are given in the name of whomever the chela calls upon. Such blessings are often passed directly from the Mahanta, the Living ECK Master to the chela. Often the blessings may be passed down by the spiritual hierarchy, and the nature of the hierarchy is complex, yet simple.

In the beginning, the SUGMAD rested quietly in ITS abode in the Ocean of Love and Mercy. Outside ITSELF there were no other planes, universes, nor worlds. Not a Soul, being, nor creature existed. Only the SUGMAD lay dreaming in ITS eternal realm. And while IT dreamed, there began the formation of the worlds inside ITSELF.

First, IT formed the Anami Lok, where dwell only the endless realms of a nameless Void. Because the SUGMAD was not pleased with this creation, IT dreamed again.

Second, IT formed the Agam Lok, where dwell only the inaccessible realms of a world where there existed

85

no life nor creatures. Because the SUGMAD was not pleased with this creation, IT dreamed again.

Third, IT formed the Hukikat Lok, where dwells the first accessible realm for beings, Souls, and entities. But because the SUGMAD was not pleased with this creation, IT dreamed again.

Fourth, IT formed the Alaya Lok, where dwell the endless worlds of no-thing. These came to be called the Sach Khand planes. Because the SUGMAD was not pleased with this creation, IT dreamed again.

Fifth, IT formed the Alakh Lok, where dwell the invisible worlds where no creature, no being, and no thing is ever seen. Therefore, it was called the invisible plane. Because the SUGMAD was not pleased with this creation, IT dreamed again.

Sixth, IT formed the Atma plane, where now dwells the Soul of everything in repose. It is here that the SUGMAD became wise in ITS judgment about the worlds to come.

The SUGMAD slept in ITS abode in the Ocean of Love and Mercy, but IT was not pleased with what IT had created. So IT dreamed more to understand what IT had formed in these planes.

Again IT awoke and looked out over the vast firmaments, wondering what belonged in them. IT dreamed again and sent ITS voice rolling through these vast worlds upon worlds. ITS voice became the heavenly music and spoke the Word which rolled through all the magnificent planes. The Word of the SUGMAD became the ECK, the Spirit of all existence. Out of this came the lords, rulers, Souls, and all beings which the SUGMAD had dreamed.

And out of this also came ITS son, the Mahanta, the consciousness of all heavenly bliss. There were then the SUGMAD, the ECK, and the Mahanta, all of which were the one great Reality.

The Lord spoke unto the Mahanta and said, "I have created the worlds of bliss and happiness. Yet there is spiritual immaturity in all my creatures. Therefore, I must create the lower order of worlds, the planes of matter, space, energy, and time. The worlds where there is shadow, light, and embodiments."

The SUGMAD stretched ITS hands over all the firmaments and created the worlds of the Triloki, which consists of the four regions between the negative pole of creation and the Atma Lok.

Within these regions IT placed the elements of matter, energy, space, and time. Here the SUGMAD created the law that nothing could exist except in relation to its opposite, called the law of polarity. Without time there could be no space, without mountains there could be no valleys. Without shadows there could be no light, and without evil there could be no good. Nor could there be ignorance without wisdom, or age without youth.

But the SUGMAD was not yet pleased with what IT had created, so closing ITS eyes IT dreamed again. This time IT formed the Spiritual Hierarchy of all the universes.

The Hierarchy began with the SUGMAD, followed by the ECK, and the Mahanta. After this came the Living ECK Master, the Adepts of the Order of the Vairagi, the lords of each plane within the higher worlds, the guardians of the Shariyat-Ki-Sugmad, and then the lower worlds were formed for those entities named the Atma, or Soul.

Over these worlds, which are three in number, IT placed Kal Niranjan, the lord of all the negative worlds. With this, IT formed the Kal force, which originated and flows out of the Niranjan as its source. Subordinate to the ECK, the Kal, however, takes precedence over all life in the lower worlds. But it is still subject to the will of the SUGMAD.

The SUGMAD was not pleased with what had been

done in ITS lower worlds so IT slept again and dreamed. Out of this dream came the lords of the lower worlds. Next the Lords of Karma were formed, the devas (angels), the planetary spirits, bruts, elementals, man, and all the creatures subordinate to him—the fish, the animals, reptiles, plants, and stones.

All these were formed on the many planes of the lower worlds; the stars, planets, and the material worlds of matter, energy, space, and time. Then the SUGMAD slept again and dreamed that all ITS manifestations needed life, so the ECK was sent into all the universes and worlds to create activity.

With this the SUGMAD gave all the worlds ITS highest creation, the Atma. The Atma, or Soul, had to be perfected so It was sent into the worlds below, only to return to Its true home when perfect.

Upon each plane the SUGMAD placed a governor, or ruler, who was to act as ITS channel for the powerful energies flowing out from the Ocean of Love and Mercy.

In the beginning, when the Supreme Deity wished to bring the universe into being, ITS first step was to create the first focus of action. This can be said to be the first step downward to the nether world.

The first focus of action was the ruler of the Anami plane, named the Anami Purusha. This is the lord of the first world, a being so mighty that its very presence is beyond the imagination of man. It was brought into existence as the first individual manifestation of the Supreme One. All subsequent creations of life embodiments were now to be carried on through this first individual manifestation.

The supreme creative ECK energy, working through the Anami Purusha, brought into existence the mighty being of the Agam Lok plane, the Agam Purusha. Through him came the Hukikat Lok and its lord, the Hukikat

Purusha. Again through this great being, the SUGMAD formed the Alaya Purusha, who became the lord of the Alaya Lok. The Alakh Purusha was the next individual manifestation of the SUGMAD, and working through him, the sixth lord, the Sat Purusha or Sat Nam of the Atma Lok, was individualized.

The Sat Nam was appointed to carry on all creative activity below that division of worlds known as the lower planes, consisting of the Etheric (Saguna Brahm), Mental (Par Brahm), Causal (Brahmanda), Astral (Anda, or Turiya Pad), and the Physical (Pinda).

The region of the Atma Lok is the Sach Khand. Sat Nam, the lord of this world, carries on all creative activity below. IT created each region. At the same time each region was created, the lords of each were created and assumed charge of their respective planes.

Over all these lower worlds Kal Niranjan was given the responsibility of exercising the power of the negative force. This Kal force was formed to have the strength to give life and body forms for each Atma which came to live in these negative worlds.

First IT formed the Saguna Lok, the upper division of the mind world. Over this he placed the ruler Saguna Brahm. He has jurisdiction over all entities and beings living on this plane.

Second IT formed the Maha Kal Lok, the mind world. Over this he placed the Par Brahm whose duties were to make all seekers of God believe this was the top of the worlds, the final resting place. It performs this duty well for many believe, upon reaching the Maha Kal Lok, that they at last have come to the true home, the abode of the Almighty.

Third, IT formed the Brahmanda Lok, the world of the causal plane. Here IT placed all the karma and recalls of Souls which reincarnated from life to life on the physical plane. Over this world he placed the Brahm, whose mighty features make one wonder if this is God. Brahm is the deity that the lower world religions all think is the SUGMAD, the Lord of Lords. Their mistake is in the illusion established by Kal Niranjan.

Fourth, IT established the Turiya Pad Lok, the astral world. Over this region he placed the Niranjan as King of all entities and beings. This is the world where Soul gets Its training in perfection so that It may return to the heavenly states again. The Niranjan here is not the true Kal Niranjan but only an offspring.

The Order of the Vairagi, which is the secret legion of ECK Adepts, was now able to establish ITS work on the many different planes of the universes of universes.

At the head of the Order is the Mahanta, the living embodiment of God. As the Mahanta, the Living ECK Master serves in the world of matter, energy, space, and time, called the physical universe. He is responsible only to the SUGMAD.

All the Adepts of the Order of the Vairagi are under him, until he relinquishes the Rod of ECK power and passes on to another plane of existence. He is the manifestation of all the spiritual essence of God, that which selects a physical embodiment and uses that body while serving in this world of matter. The worlds over which he rules are every plane from the Ocean of Love and Mercy to the lowest of the physical universe. He functions equally upon every plane in the Atma Sarup, and uses the physical body as the instrument to serve in the physical worlds.

He places these magnificent Adepts in charge of the Shariyat-Ki-Sugmad, the Holy Book of the ECK Order. They are the guardians of these works, and upon each plane an Adept of the Order of the Vairagi is in charge of a section of this Book of Golden Wisdom. A section

90

of the book is within the Temple of Golden Wisdom on each plane as designated by the SUGMAD.

The planes and guardians are:

1. The Ocean of Love and Mercy—the SUGMAD.

2. The Anami Lok—the Padma Samba is the guardian of this section of the Shariyat-Ki-Sugmad. It is kept in the Temple of Golden Wisdom known as the Sata Visic Palace.

3. The Agam Lok—the Adept here is the Mahaya Guru, guardian of the Holy Book at the Kazi Dawtz Temple of Golden Wisdom.

4. The Hukikat Lok—the Adept here is the Asanga Kaya, the guardian of the Holy Book at the Jartz Chong Temple of Golden Wisdom.

5. The Alaya Lok—the Adept here is the great Tsong Sikhsa, guardian of the Holy Book at the Anakamudi Temple of Golden Wisdom.

6. The Alakh Lok—the Adept here is the Sokagampo, guardian of the Holy Book at the Tamanata Kop Temple of Golden Wisdom.

7. The Atma Lok—the Adept here is the Jagat Giri, guardian of the Holy Book at the Param Akshar Temple of Golden Wisdom. This is the house of imperishable knowledge. It is the highest that Soul can go, as long as It is attached to a physical body, to study at any of the Temples of Golden Wisdom.

8. In the worlds below the Atma plane (where the Shariyat-Ki-Sugmad is kept for those who are able to study its golden pages) is the Saguna Lok (etheric world). The Adept here is Lai Tsi, guardian of the Holy Book at the Dayaka Temple of Golden Wisdom in the city of Arhirit.

9. The Par Brahm Lok (Mental world)—the Adept here is the Koji Chanda, guardian of the Holy Book at the Namayatan Temple of Golden Wisdom in the city of Mer Kailash.

10. The Brahmanda Lok (Causal world)—the Adept here is Shamus-i-Tabriz, guardian of the Holy Book at the Sakapori Temple of Golden Wisdom in the city of Honu.

11. The Anda Lok (Astral world)—the Adept here is Gopal Das, guardian of the Holy Book of the Askleposis Temple of Golden Wisdom in the city of Sahasra-Dal-Kanwal.

12. The Pinda Lok (Physical world)—the Adept here is Rami Nuri, guardian of the Holy Book at the Moksha Temple of Golden Wisdom in the city of Retz, Venus.

13. The Prithvi Lok (Earth world)—the Adept here is Yaubl Sacabi, guardian of the Holy Book at the Gare-Hira Temple of Golden Wisdom at Agam Des, the home of the Eshwar-Khanewale (the God-eaters) in the Himalayan mountains.

14. The Surati Lok (Mountain world)—the Adept here is Fubbi Quantz, guardian of the Holy Book at the Katsupari Monastery Temple of Golden Wisdom in northern Tibet.

15. The Asurati Lok (Desert world)—the Adept here is Banjani, guardian of the Holy Book at the Faqiti Monastery Temple of Golden Wisdom in the Gobi Desert. The section here is only an introduction to the Shariyat-Ki-Sugmad. Chelas are usually taken here to begin their study of the holy works in the dream state.

The Mahanta is the Godman, the ancient one who reincarnates again and again in the world of matter. He comes in every age, every lifetime, to gather up those who have failed to accept him in the past. All who have surrendered to him in any particular life and accept him as the Living ECK Master work out all karma before their translation from the body.

The Mahanta is the father of all who have studied with him in the past. During each incarnation he takes on another body and personality. Those who have followed

92

him in the past and have reincarnated again will always find the Mahanta. They will come to learn that all who follow the path of ECK are the chosen people of God.

The Mahanta is the Avatar of his time. He is concerned only with the spiritual development of all Souls. He takes care of karma and helps to resolve it for those who come under his guidance on the path of ECK. He also takes care of the karmic pattern of the human race, and all life within this universe upon whatever planet it may be and also the life that exists on the other planes within the God Worlds. He does all this individually and collectively. He uplifts all Souls no matter what plane they may be upon.

He is in all places at the same time because he is Spirit, the ECK. By this very reason he is able to be with all who follow the path of the holy science of ECK. He has nothing to do with psychic phenomena nor will he perform miracles merely because someone requests that he do so. He appears to those in danger to warn them and will take care of all the chelas of ECK.

There is only one to whom the Mahanta bows in humble submission. This is the Supreme Lord, the SUGMAD. ITS sovereign will is the only law the Mahanta recognizes, and the universal law of all laws—love. While living on earth in the human form though he will break no law of man, but supports all good governments. His life and works are universal. He does not belong to any race or time, but to all nations and all times. Correctly, he is a citizen of the macrocosmic worlds, a being which has entered this world to bring the Light to all peoples.

The Mahanta is generally a family man—he is never an ascetic nor does he ever encourage austerities. He will advocate keeping the body healthy, as it is his duty to serve the world.

The Mahanta, the Living ECK Master lives in the world

although he is not of it. He has come to help all those who desire it, and enters the stream of humanity to give this help. Yet he himself stands aloof from the waves of human passions. He has attained all virtues. He believes in the highest degree of strength; spiritual strength which cannot be separated from the moral qualities of mankind. This strength is the strength of love. He is stronger than any man in intellect or spirit, for he has unlimited power, and yet this strength is combined with the noble virtues of the humble and gentle. All people find in him inspiration for the development of noble character.

In the realm of religion the Mahanta is a paradox. He has no theology. He teaches none, yet he is the greatest religious leader on earth. The system of ECK, which he teaches, is not an orthodox religion although it leads to the most complete and enlightening religious experience. He is universal in all the teachings of ECK. Not having a creedlike religion, he never deliberately antagonizes any creed, sect, or religious institution.

He never finds fault with anyone or anything, but draws the line sharply between God and Kal. To correct errors in the chelas the Mahanta often points out the opposite virtues, frequently in examples.

The Mahanta is omnipresent, all-pervading, except in his physical limitations. Spiritually he has no limitation, but the body is not the Mahanta. It is only a covering of one of his instruments. He can leave the body and work on any of the spiritual planes at his own volition. He has no limitations being one with the SUGMAD.

All the Living ECK Masters have taught, "I and the SUGMAD are one." In the process of the development of the Mahanta, all Living ECK Masters, in their days on earth, wore the mantle of the Mahanta and expanded their Godlike qualities in common with all men. The Living ECK Master is, therefore, the divine man; a real son of

94

God. Yet every man has in him the latent possibilities for the same expansion to mastership. He only requires the Living ECK Master to help develop it.

When the Master gains Mahantaship he attains conscious oneness with the SUGMAD. This is the distinguishing quality of the Living ECK Master. He knows his relationship with the SUGMAD, and is able to consciously exercise his powers as a son of God. He is literally part of the all-embracing ECK, partaking of Its qualities, and is the chief instrument which the Supreme Being uses in ITS universes. IT gives ITS boundless love to all mankind through the Mahanta.

A vital difference exists between the Mahanta and a departed Master. The chela cannot follow a Master who has left this plane and gone into the other worlds. The departed one cannot initiate anyone on the spiritual path. He has nothing now to do with the earth world. Neither can anyone follow two or more Masters at the same time. Here one is following only principles in the light of the universal cause, but not the Living ECK Master.

No child can get nourishment from a deceased mother, nor a sick man from a departed doctor. The Masters of the past ages have left this field of action and so their work here is finished. Neither does one follow a book because it is said to be truth. No man can get truth out of a book. It must come out of himself. Therefore, all who wish the truth of ECK must follow the Mahanta, the Living ECK Master. The SUGMAD cannot instruct, or give man the needed help on the upward path, without the Mahanta in human form to act as his instrument and spokesman. The greatest stumbling block for man is that he cannot see all God's manifestations.

Those who cling to a Master who has been translated from this earth world are in error. He is not dead, but he has left the field of action in this region of matter. He is no longer in touch with humanity; his work is elsewhere. The discipleship of the chela must change to the successor.

Men must recognize that feelings provide no proof in religious matters. The Mahanta will try to teach the chela to discount feelings as proofs of religious dogma. Only the Living ECK Master can offer the chela a definite method by which he can prove all things for himself.

There is one way to know the Living ECK Master is authentic. That is to see him on some higher plane where assumption is impossible. If the Mahanta is seen in his radiant form, the chela knows this is the true Master of ECKANKAR. It is only when the chela is ready that he will see the Mahanta in the radiant form.

Whenever the chela finds the Living ECK Master he should follow him with unwavering faith and determination and accept him wholeheartedly. If the chela runs up against karma and burdens, he must hold a steady hand on himself and wait while these are being worked out by the ECK Master.

Hold all and wait. The questions that are in one's mind will be worked out eventually without a word from the Master. The light becomes stronger and the darkness vanishes in the reorganization of the inner man and his thinking processes and habits. Do not make the mistake of trying to fit the teachings of ECK into the old ways of thinking. Drop all and start over again.

It is not possible to enter into the Kingdom of Heaven except through the teachings of ECKANKAR. The path lies with the Mahanta and all who come to him will have salvation and liberation from worldly affairs. Unless Soul does this and follows the path of ECK with loving obedience, it is impossible for It to enter into the Ocean of Love and Mercy and become a Co-worker with God.

Each Soul that becomes a chela of the living Mahanta starts working out Its karma for permanent entry into the Kingdom of Heaven. If It is initiated, this is assured for all karma will be resolved and the Lords of Karma will never again bother him at the end of his earthly existence. When he enters into the next world, should it be on one of the lower planes by the will of the Mahanta, he must work off his karma on that plane. Should it be on the Astral Plane, he must stay for a period until his astral karma is worked off. This is true of every plane below the Atma region. However, the ECK initiate of the Second Circle will rise above any of these lower worlds upon the decease of the physical vehicle. He will enter into the Atma world at once, escorted by the living Mahanta.

However, if any Soul who is a chela or initiate leaves the path of ECK for another way to the heavenly worlds during any particular embodiment on earth, he must expect his karma to be extended. His karmic burden increases as he gathers more, going through incarnation after incarnation searching blindly for what he has given up. Not knowing, not seeing that the Kal Niranjan has blinded his eyes to the glory of the heavenly worlds.

He cannot leave the path of ECK expecting to find salvation and liberation in the Prithvi Lok (Earth world). No one but the living Mahanta can take him out of this plane of matter. He will again someday meet with the Living ECK Master, when ready, and enter permanently into the Kingdom of Heaven.

Woe be to him who tries to travel another path of religious doctrine or spiritual works while at the same time a chela of the Living ECK Master. He will suffer the penalties of his folly and not know what has created his adversities. If he becomes an initiate in ECKANKAR there shall be no wavering from the path unless he wishes an adverse life and falling into disgrace. If he accepts titles, rewards, and so-called benefits from others who are not

97

on the path of ECK there will also be the same adversities of life.

He must have that burning faith in the ECK in order to find the liberation of Soul. He must never allow anything to disturb this and take him away from the path. If he should try to enhance and advance a teaching of the lower order, or another order at the same time he is following the path of ECK, there will be little spiritual unfoldment for him.

The ECKist recognizes no other religion, although such exists in this physical world. Nor does he recognize any metaphysical teaching, occultism, or any world theological faiths, creeds, and cults, all of which claim to be the way to God. The ECKist, however, does not condemn any of these because they are, in a sense, all under ECK as each has its origin in the ECK. These are only the chelas of the Living ECK Master who have strayed from the path and established a faith of their own. It is like the shadow of truth. Whoever wants the shadow instead of the Light is foolish.

Man will take to religion, even if he has to invent one. The weak need the support, and although it is an illusionary product in the spirit-matter worlds, it shall not be taken from man. Every man must seek the path of ECK for himself, and walk upon it for himself.

A spiritual darkness will brood over the world and all men who walk upon the surface of the earth will be sick from it. Except for the Satya Yuga, the Golden Age, there is a physical and moral deterioration of man in all other yugas. Moral corruption eats into the vitals of the human race and none but those who follow the path of ECK are immune to it. Practically every man, except the ECKist, is lost in the dense forests of morality because each is blind. He suffers from spiritual amnesia for there is no memory nor recollection of his true home.

In addition to this mental and spiritual plight, many suffer from physical illness, heartbreak, and are otherwise worn and weary. They fumble and stumble not knowing where to find the Living ECK Master. They pray to their God but there is little answer. Each is looking for miracles that can happen, provided they recognize the Master is waiting for each and all.

The entire human race is but an aggregation of driven slaves from childhood to old age while cares and anxieties multiply. They wait only for death, and this death is the doorway into the Kingdom of Heaven. The human race is told by the priests and religious fanatics that death is the mystery. But for the ECKist there is no mystery in the phenomena of death for he practices dying daily and visiting the heavenly worlds. When the time comes for this phenomena to take place in the Pinda world, it is found that he can leave the body under his own volition.

The ECK Initiate is dead in the Physical body, but always alive in the Atma Sarup. Thus each man needs to know himself as Soul, living in the body of the ECK (spirit). He must realize that he is not the physical vehicle, that it is only an outer garment used for protection against the coarse vibrations of the lower worlds.

The chela is never converted in ECK. Conversion is not a part of the works of ECKANKAR. He is transformed and transmuted instead to the body of ECK. He repents of karma, that is, gives up the Kal and accepts the Mahanta as his spiritual guide. This is the ECK side, and there is always the factor of total surrender of the human consciousness to the Mahanta. This is not an emotional (astral) experience.

Any man who makes claims that he is a master, adept, or savior of the human race and still speaks of being an incarnation of a past life is false in his claims. Only the Living ECK Master can truly say that he is the Ancient

One, the incarnation of the ECK (Spirit) and the Mahanta Consciousness. No others can make this claim.

The chela must learn that cleanliness of the mind and body is a necessity in the works of ECK. He must take care of his body, keep it clean at all times, see that his hair and his face are properly trimmed, and that it is free of odors. He must keep his mind free from the pollution of worldly affairs, such as lust, anger, greed, attachment to worldly desires, and vanity. These are the five passions of the mind. But he cannot allow them to infest his mind for they will in turn infest the body.

The laws and rules for the ECK chela are simple. These are to give harmony, purity, and perfection of Soul. This constitutes heaven while in the physical vehicle. One can discern this heavenly state in the proportion that he relinquishes the false concepts of the limited, mortal consciousness of man. He must yield himself, the inner self, to the one divine ECK. Peace and well-being then enters into his human experience of life.

He who enters into the works of ECKANKAR becomes an Acolyte. He is put under the spiritual discipline of ECK, prior to his true induction into the invisible order. He is a probationer who must prove his worth before entering into the true works of ECKANKAR.

He must practice the disciplines of ECK. The first is to have cleanliness of mind, that no words which would pollute the air enter into his mind. He shall look upon all men as creatures of God and this only; for they, like himself, are temples who shall eventually become Co-workers with God.

He must, in mind, fast continuously from all Kal thoughts which could infect his mental state and consciousness. Through this he learns the powerful awareness of the presence of the Living ECK Master, who is with him constantly. He learns not to be deceived or dismayed by the conflicting world around him. He knows that all universes, regardless of whether or not they are under the rulership of the Kal Niranjan, are really worlds of perfection, harmony, and good.

He learns that patience is the greatest discipline of all the spiritual works of ECK. By patience he can endure life, hardships, karmic burdens, the slanders of men, and the pricks of pain and disease. He keeps his mind steadfastly upon the Light of God, never swerving, never letting up on his attention to the goal of God-Realization.

He comes to know humility and chastity in his life on earth and that all his responsibility belongs to God, not to anyone nor anything within this physical realm. His loved ones, family, and relatives are the images of God, mirrored in this worldly life and embodiment to serve the SUGMAD, the Supreme Deity.

He soon learns that humility is opposite to Kani, the ego. He will not let this false concept of his worth to the Master and to the SUGMAD stand in his way to reach the heavenly states. He knows that vanity is only a trap of Kal Niranjan and that he will become a fool if he lets himself be enslaved by Kal.

He will come to discriminate between all things, that there is no good nor evil, no beauty nor ugliness, and there is no sin. That all these are concepts of the mind, the dual forces in the matter worlds. Once he recognizes and understands this, he will then be free of all the Kal traps.

He will be ready to enter into the Kingdom of God, the Ocean of Love and Mercy.

He will be the ECK, of Itself.

6

The
Living ECK Master

The Living ECK Master is always higher on the spiritual scale of God than any saints of the worldly religions. Since the majority of these Masters have been the Living ECK Master of their respective sojourn in this world, it means that each in his time was the direct manifestation of God; the divine channel which God uses as ITS voice to speak to the worlds within ITSELF.

Hence, the Living ECK Master is omniscient, omnipotent, and omnipresent. Each who has served his respective time in the worlds of God, including the physical plane, is known as the Mahanta, the Vi-Guru, the highest of all spiritual Masters throughout the universes of the SUGMAD. None are higher than the Mahanta for he alone possesses the shining consciousness of the SUGMAD.

The saints of the various religions have never been placed in the same category. Therefore, they should never be considered in the same distinctive class as the Living ECK Master. All that is said here is that those whose training has been in the traditional religious manner would possibly resist this statement of golden truth. Truth has never been told in the physical worlds. It has been hidden from the eyes and ears of the profane by those who wish to make slaves of the masses. It has only been a control factor in the managing of men to keep their attention riveted upon one particular religious object; this is the foundation of the religions of the world that claim to have Truth. There is no basis for this consideration, and that is what it is, a consideration of the worst sort.

Truth is no being's prerogative nor any religion's singular strength. Since everything in this physical universe is controlled by Kal Niranjan (the negative power), we have nothing that can say it represents the ultimate in the perfect sense, except ECKANKAR.

Since the ECK is the original, primitive source of all life, It is closer to Truth than any orthodox religion, philosophy, or church. Those who point fingers at ECK, claiming that here are false teachings taught by false prophets, are not aware that they are themselves misled by the Kal. None of these detractors are enlightened with Truth. They can quote only from the sacred books of their representative religions strictly stating their own interpretations. None have any further advancement than the Astral worlds and usually the lower planes of this first region beyond the physical senses.

Neither do they have any experience in the ECK Life-Sound Current. Few, if any, can do anything more than preach the message of Kal. They are the agents of the Kal, establishing the delusion that their purpose is to give out truth, but this truth is that of the negative power. Theirs is the message of the Universal Mind Power.

Kal agents promise more abundant life in the name of their saviors. They give the impression that nothing is greater than their own words. This illusion is furthered by the fact that life somehow always manages to upset any faith they have in their gods.

This brings about disappointment, frustrations, and unhappiness. It never gives any glimpse of the true reality. Nor does it bring enlightenment, or knowledge of survival of Soul. Like the donkey with a carrot dangling before its nose to keep it moving, forever out of reach, the man who follows these Kal teachings goes through life with false hopes. For hope is all he has, and never faith.

The Living ECK Master points out again and again that each man can have the joy of immortality if he follows the words of the ECK. No other religions or masters can give the complete Truth except the Living ECK Master, who is the Mahanta, the resurrected Spirit of God, the ECK, serving all Souls in every universe of God.

While he serves out his mission as the Mahanta, he has to do duty not only upon the earth and every planet, star, and constellation in the material world, but in every plane within the universe of God's universe. Hence, he is the Living ECK Master and the Mahanta to every Soul, regardless of where that entity may be living. Whether It be in hell or the Ocean of Love and Mercy, the Mahanta is with It, as well as with all other Souls. The Soul only has to recognize this to understand and know this miracle of life.

All others who claim they are the messengers, preachers, or the voice of God do so for some materialistic motive. But the Mahanta has none; he serves God; he is the servant of God; he is the servant of the servants of the Lord because he has been selected and given the command. His life is so directed that even in the physical world he does not accept anything from life but always gives to those who seek him out.

Yet, woe to those who take advantage of his generosity and his efforts to give. These are the false followers, the seekers of the material things of life, the parasites who

105

attempt to feed upon the ECK which flows out of the Mahanta, the perfect instrument of God.

Man is apt to be this way and will oft seek out the Mahanta to pour out his woes and personal issues. He asks for everything, and in return for resolving his problems and for success or materialistic gains, he promises his faith, everlasting devotion, dedication, gratitude, and his payment in monetary means. These are only insincere promises for the Mahanta knows that when a solicitor has received his gift from God, via the Living ECK Master, he generally forgets in his joy to offer his gift. He honestly intends to fulfill his promise of payment, but the Kal activities stir within him and again his desire for physical well-being becomes greater than his longing for God.

This longing is forgotten in his workaday life in the material world. He seeks love and comfort by every possible means, and those metaphysicians and doctors of the mind and Soul who promise him a kingdom on earth are only false prophets.

If they promise him rewards in heaven after life here on earth, this, too, is a series of false promises. The kingdom of the ECK is so far beyond this world that few, if any, recognize the life which they can have if only they would follow the path of the ECK Truths.

If the Mahanta bestows gifts upon the solicitor, then he is the most fortunate of the fortunates for it means that he basks in the favor of the Living ECK Master and seeks nothing further in life. He has met and found the true Vi-Guru, and must now start his spiritual journey to God.

All Souls struggling to find their way to the true path of God—the way of ECKANKAR—will eventually seek out the Living ECK Master. Each will come to know that life itself is the elemental part of ECK, and it is only because of the will of the SUGMAD that all Souls have existence.

All religions have had a beginning and an ending. Whenever the history of the human race is examined it is found that many religions have existed on the physical planes, but few have lasted beyond a thousand years. All world religions, therefore, are materialistic in nature and worship the wrong power, the wrong God. Unless a religion has for its basic teaching the Living ECK Master, the Sound Current, and the Light, it will not have longevity. Few, if any, religions have such elements in their teachings.

It is the will of God that Souls have existence. This is the doctrine of the ECK, the way of Truth. No man comes to the SUGMAD except through the Mahanta. Life has no existence but for the love and mercy of God. Only Soul can have life because IT (God) has willed it to be.

The man who solicits the gifts of God for health, monetary means, and worldly love, only keeps the ECK from entering into him and healing all aspects of his life. To ask is never to receive, to question is to defeat one's own purpose with God, and to make promises which knowingly are false is to annul one's advancement on the spiritual path.

To ridicule, to scorn, to speak mockingly of the words of the Mahanta, and not to have faith in him and the cause of ECK is to bring woes on the advocator of doubt. It brings his karmic progress to a halt, increases his incarnations in this world, and causes him to suffer untold hardships.

The ignorant and the naive will never understand, nor shall they learn except by experiencing the slow death brought about by their own overt acts against the Mahanta and the ECK. This is actually creating overt acts against the SUGMAD.

Self-assertion, self-righteousness, self-will, and self-seeking at the expense of the ECK, likewise, brings untold hardships of life for one who indulges in these things during his life in the spirito-materialistic worlds. Not only does this occur for him in the physical world, but upon every plane of existence. He who takes up such Kalistic virtues is never at peace with himself. But he shall become like a fine crystal globe, to ping just right would cause it to break into a thousand pieces. No man should wish this upon himself but should seek God for ITSELF, and never for any personal motivation.

Religion speaks of peace after death for man. But this is only a lower-world teaching. It is not true, but only a promise to keep man happy, a promise that he is going to be free of the trials and tribulations of this earthly life. But not until Soul has gained the realization of the SUGMAD shall he become peaceful and have harmony with all life. This is possible not only after death, but while he is still living in the physical embodiment.

The chela keeps wondering when he will reach that moment of meeting with God. But it will never come for, if he would realize it, he is already at that moment. Rather, he is at this focal point in eternity for the SUGMAD is always with him, in the form of the Living ECK Master. The chela is always in the present for the present is always eternity. God is with him all the time as the Living ECK Master, every moment of his life.

Therefore, the chela should recognize that if God is with him, then the Living ECK Master is always the presence he experiences constantly. He should understand this and have it written upon his heart, for the Mahanta is the vehicle God uses to reach every Soul who will listen. This should be kept in mind constantly.

Privacy is a necessity in the life of every ECK Master. He must have it or he cannot give the inner service to mankind as he should. But with the way men try to use him for their own means and motivation, he generally has little privacy and much less rest.

The chela must be dedicated to the ECK. Dedication is his greatest asset. He must give this dedication to the Mahanta, the Living ECK Master because he is the only manifestation of God that can be recognized by those in the human state of consciousness. If the chela is not possessed of this quality of dedication and loyalty to the path of ECK, his incarnations are lengthened in this world, and he shall not be able to enter into the next worlds at the end of his present life.

The Living ECK Master is not a therapist, as understood in the physical world, nor at any time does he pose as one. If the chela or the nonchela considers him as such, they are defeating their own purpose. He is a healer, one who can read the auras of chelas and others, one who knows the past, present, and future of the human race. But he is not a therapist, nor a fortune-teller, nor a finder of lost articles. He is none of these things, but a manifestation of God upon earth. He is a miracle worker, but never attempts to prove himself when called upon to do so. He does not perform wonders simply because someone challenges him to do so. He will not perform magic nor give himself over to tricks as many believe he should do. But he proves himself in mysterious ways to everyone. He gives of himself and is forgiving of all others. He never considers anything, nor anyone, as an enemy. He knows that it is the Kal Niranjan who is trying to defeat him, but this is the way of God.

He points this out to all who question him and say that he should bring his mighty powers into action to be rid of Kal Niranjan. He does not battle, nor destroy anything that is a creature of God, for the Kal is also part of God's own divine power put here to act as the purifying

109

agent for all Souls.

The Mahanta, therefore, allows all things to have their freedom. He gives each power through God because this is the way of life and must be done in accordance with God's will.

The trouble with religion is that one individual appears in what might be a perfect manifestation of God, and so begins a worship of that manifestation. Most of these manifestations are only social, Astral, or Mental phenomena and they deceive the worshiper.

Such an individual is but a man-made object, established by the Kal power to give man something to keep his mind from Truth. This is the way of all orthodox religions.

Orthodox religious leaders appear to follow out this trend because of the difference on thought, and worship of their respective desires.

This is all because few, if any, realize what they are trying to establish in the field of worship. It is simply a crude manifestation which is little more than a symbol with considerations pouring into it and impressing the mind so that it will stay with men until the end of their earthly time.

Most religions have been rewritten again and again and reinterpreted until there is little vitality of the primitive teachings left anywhere in any worldly path. When a religion begins to lose its force in this world, it gradually dies away as all have in the present and past.

Thus, the ECK is the true faith. Its teachings are from the ancient original source, pure and unadulterated in ITS message. It is direct from God in ITS Ocean of Love and Mercy, and is given through the pure vehicle, the true instrument, the Mahanta, and is the highest message of the SUGMAD.

The Master always presents the straight path to God,

but it is the chela's relationship with the human element in others that manages to upset and divert the Master's way to heaven. Or it is man's relationship with himself which brings about the ingredients of human problems on the physical level of life.

The Living ECK Master strives constantly to take the chela out of the earthly games level but he never makes rules nor rituals, never lays down laws and proclaims his way to God as the better way, although all know it is. He knows that all worldly religions are pseudo and in the minority, but he seldom states this in any of his works. He never asks that anyone follow his path and abide by his own conduct and words. He knows that many men cannot do this as they have established their own consciousness in orthodox religion and will be offended should he demand they follow him.

All worldly religions are for the benefit of the leader. The Living ECK Master teaches all who listen to his word that it is Truth and the chela must learn to separate Truth from false teachings. Until the chela has learned to do this he is apt to wander about in this world of mind and body through centuries of reincarnations.

The Living ECK Master is above civilization and culture. He knows that all there is in this world is life and embodiments. These are forms with which he seldom, if at any time, has any relationship. He works only through each Soul, which is the divine spark of life within each embodiment.

The Mahanta is always born near or on a large body of water. His birth is always mysterious and men of ordinary birth do not know his origin. Nor does any man know who his sires might be, their true names or their true origin.

The ECK enters into the womb of a virgin, the queen of heaven, who has submitted to the true spirit of the universe. The consciousness of the Mahanta state is planted as the seed, and carefully nurtured in the womb. When the embodiment of flesh is brought into this world, a man-child is born. It starts its unfoldment over a period of years until the state of perfection is reached, in adulthood. Then the chosen one learns that he is the Living ECK Master of his times.

There is never a time when the world is without a Mahanta, the Living ECK Master, for God manifests IT-SELF again and again in the embodiment of the chosen one. IT is constant and always in the worlds. For in the Living ECK Master does IT find perfection, as he is the true instrument for the SUGMAD, the Vi-Guru, the Love and Spirit of the SUGMAD.

All life springs from its origin in God, but manifests in the perfect body of the SUGMAD via the Mahanta. This is the living Quintan (five), or the fivefold bodies of the Mahanta. This is the greater part of the SUGMAD which is the Word made flesh in the lower worlds. The Mahanta thereby has a body which functions as an instrument of God upon each plane throughout the worlds of Spirit, including the true spiritual planes.

Therefore, the Living ECK Master has existence on every plane in the lower worlds in a body; the Physical, Astral, Causal, Mental and Soul. At the same time, he also exists in the non-body form which is the ECK. Above the Atma world (the Soul Plane), he is entirely without form and is completely omnipresent. While living in the five lower planes he is omnipresent, while at the same time existing in the Mahanta state in each world and administering to those entities and physically-embodied Souls as deemed necessary, as well as to his own chelas and initiates of ECKANKAR.

All religions born upon this earth speak of their saviors having three bodies, or three states, which are known

112

as the Trinity. These are the lower states of consciousness which millions have accepted and put their desires and ambitions into to have saving grace. ECK never speaks of any orthodox religion as being beneath the true spiritual works of God, but merely makes it known that these religions are the offshoots of ECKANKAR, the original source of all life.

All men and all entities existing in every universe of God will in time come to know each exists because God has given all life through the perfected state of ITS manifestation on earth and upon every plane in the universe. The Mahanta is ITS only manifestation, the Light of the worlds, the Voice of God, which is heard in every corner and closet of every plane. When he speaks, the Voice of God is heard. Every word that he utters is Truth to all men, entities, and creatures.

He gives life and allows the actions of every man and creature upon earth and throughout the heavens of God to do all deeds in freedom of respective consciousness. For each and all he is the vehicle of God, and he is able to give all things and be all things to all through the power of the ECK.

The Mahanta is a law unto himself. So oft does he speak of life itself as being his servant, but he commands heaven and earth, yet never does he allow himself to be worshiped perfectly as man. Only as the Mahanta, the perfect consciousness.

When Lai Tsi, the perfect ECK Master of China in the ancient days, stood upon the hill and preached the sermon that gained him the title of perfection as the Mahanta of his day, he was approached by a disciple who asked, "Master, who are you?"

"Whom do you say that I am?" Lai Tsi asked.

"You are the Mahanta, the perfect Master," said the disciple.

113

"If this is what you believe you have gained the true enlightenment of God. From this day you have entered into heaven and will be at my side."

Man earns himself a place in heaven when he recognizes the Mahanta and knows him for what he is. The world that follows the dictum of the Living ECK Master and fulfills his slightest desire does so only so it can gain for itself. The Mahanta gives, regardless of the motivation, if he knows that the gift will be a gain for the solicitor.

To knock and receive is not always the motive for the Master to fulfill a request. He who asks must gain it by earning the gift. The gift to anyone is that which God gives via the Mahanta. But it is the decision of the Mahanta as to who may receive, and who is worthy of the gift.

All may be worthy yet cannot receive the gifts of God because the heart is not ready. If one wishes to have a gift from the SUGMAD his heart must become pure and gentle. He cannot receive when filled with doubts, lust, unhappiness, and dread. Only those who are dedicated, happy, and love God are able to receive the gift of God that the Mahanta passes to each who has earned his rightful place in the heavenly kingdom.

When shorn of the time-sense, when knowledge of space has left the human consciousness, then shall the chela be relieved of the anxiety of experiencing life as a succession of problems, past, present, and future. The barriers of time and space can be broken by accepting the Mahanta as the true one, and by entering into the spiritual view of life, as the unfolding of all life is eternity. Eternity is an expression of life without a sense of time and space, already established by the SUGMAD. Once the chela surrenders to IT and accepts as valid that the ECK is the source of all life, his concepts of eternity change his human consciousness into a state of God-knowing— the divine consciousness.

114

Man's essential nature is primarily a spiritual desire for God. He must pray that the eternal ECK will visit Itself upon him, and that the living Master will appear to remove any doubt and act as his divine guide. Then all the lower aspects of human nature will be filled with the holy Light and Sound. When this divine visitation is given unto him, then does he become worthy of any gift of God and able to serve in this world as a Co-worker with the Mahanta.

Each Soul can be liberated so that It may stand upon the high summit of the spiritual mountain and view the world. This is a symbol of the understanding that each chela in ECKANKAR will reach. This is eternity—the view from the hilltop of spiritual vision. The eternal view that is seen is the wholeness of life, free from time and space of the lower worlds.

Perfection may seem far from the human state of consciousness, but one can be thankful that perfection is divinely true in the present now and not in some distant future. If one looks, he will find divine power in the human situation as well as in the spiritual situation. Man can always bring out in the human self the divine Truth. He only has to be himself.

As man deepens his understanding of the divine ECK his outlook changes. The ECK, which is the essence of God, is divine love, and being love It naturally provides only the good karma of life.

The ECK is uninterrupted, continuing, eternal. It is the reality of all life manifested here in this world in the embodiment of the Living ECK Master. When one sees beyond the views of this world, he is living in Spirit. He can avoid all the anxieties and dangers of this worldly life by lifting himself again to the top of the spiritual mountain. He looks neither to the past nor to the future, but to the present, the now, knowing that the SUGMAD lives only in the present. He knows that with each step he takes he is on hallowed ground, for the Mahanta is always with him.

The Word of God within this world has already been done. It is the state of man's consciousness which has not unfolded but will continue to unfold. The chela is ever developing and can reach the state of spiritual perfection only if he will accept and believe what is taking place in the activity of Soul.

The Living ECK Master embraces all humanity because he is the only channel that can do so. He is able to live in an enlarged state of present consciousness and few, if any, can ever do this. Certainly none of the ancients could do this, although many were able to experience the good of life. If the chela is seeking eternity then he must first look for it within his own orbit. Since the Living ECK Master is in this circle of being that is the personal and universal self of the chela, then the latter must seek it with the Living ECK Master.

Once he has established the recognition of life as it is, then the knowledge that he is immortal comes to him. He experiences the ending of all karma which has been the Kal cause and establishes only the God-given karma within the world of worlds.

Eternity is experienced by the chela in ECKANKAR when the Mahanta takes him to the top of the spiritual mountain and lets him view the scrambling activities of the little selves among the masses of humanity. From this position the view is not limited to the senses of the human consciousness and there is no time-space sense. All below him are desperately trying to scramble up the mountainside to the summit where the view is eternal and the spiritual atmosphere is clear. To live in the world of humanity, as the chela must do until the end of his days in the physical embodiment, he must constantly dwell on the spiritual summits of God.

Soul is the all-inclusive consciousness of the individual established in God, and outside the concepts of the aspects of the lower worlds. It has been named static but It is not this, for Soul is dynamic within the worlds of God ITSELF. It is a state of awareness which experiences life through the spiritual senses. The spiritual senses are able to have perception, conception, and realization.

Man consists only of Soul. There is nothing else which can give the physical self life. He has body, mind, and Soul. He is Soul but has not yet recognized this. His spiritual senses have not yet been activated so he does not know Soul is the only thing he is in eternity.

Soul is a spark of the divine ECK. It has three attributes with the SUGMAD, i.e. a perception of eternity through inner sight, hearing, and knowing, but mainly knowingness; It has conception of all that It gathers in through the inner senses, that is an understanding of what has been seen, heard, and known; It recognizes or realizes Its relationship with God through God-Realization, Self-Realization, and Mind-Realization. Soul realizes that It is part of the whole of ECK, not with God. As a divine spark of the ECK, It can have a realization that It is the ECK Itself. No man or Soul has ever, in the true state, felt that he or It was whole with God.

It is through these attributes that Soul controls the body which It occupies during any given time in the world of matter. The control of the body and environment depends on the strength and realization that It has gained through these three attributes. This again depends on the degree of Its awakened consciousness. This is an explanation of why each man is different from another. This is also in accordance with the law of evolution which establishes inequality in all things and beings and their continued effort for spiritual unfoldment.

117

The Mahanta is not only the Living ECK Master, but a living example of the philosophy of ECKANKAR, the high priest and a fountain of knowledge for ECK. He is one who knows divine law, government of the heavenly worlds, and the workings of the human mind and Soul, as well as the art of spiritual healing, magic, prophecy, and miracles.

The love of the Living ECK Master for all chelas is on the highest plane and should not be considered in any other manner. When the gift of love is passed to the chela he should be contented, for it has been his privilege to gain the inner heights through the Mahanta. If the chela is happy in this then the reality of God shall be his own realization.

It is best not to make contact with the Living ECK Master in the physical but through the inner level, for all comes as the secret teachings from the heart of the Mahanta to each chela under his protection and guidance. This is the inner way and all who come unto the Mahanta shall be lifted up into heaven.

ECK is always at war with Kal Niranjan, and all the orthodox religions and mass societies and civilizations created by the Kal. Therefore, orthodox religions and the masses have always tried to hinder the progress of the ECK in the lower worlds.

Those who follow the Kal are mainly interested in the effects of materialistic power. The subtle play of the Kal is an intricate working of power forces among the various minor forces in these worlds of its own.

Yet on the opposing side all the power of God must reach these worlds through the perfect instrument of the Mahanta, the Living ECK Master. There is no other way, for he is the distributor of the power. All may see the example of this in the material life here on earth in the same manner, and they recognize that each within himself is a distributor of this power which gives life and creation to their environment.

The Living ECK Master is appointed to his high position and is expected to defend the God-power, and to defend the works of ECK and the chelas who have put their interest in ECK. The Living ECK Master is not allowed to retire from his field of action in this life until another is ready and trained to replace him.

When the Living ECK Master's position is attacked by revolt, or by dissatisfaction among the followers of ECK, he will defend himself. Not in the way many would expect, but in ways that few can recognize. The defense will come from the inner planes, and by means of the ECK. Those who revolt or become dissatisfied cannot bring about any attack upon the Living ECK Master or his position in life. If they do, there is always the swiftest of retribution, which is not always recognized by the receiver nor those who might have observed the occasion.

Those who are the children of ECK are the sons and daughters of the divine Sound Current. They are the heroic people of their age, and they could suffer at the hands of the orthodox who wish to keep the doctrine of the ECK from spreading.

Man cannot receive any more than he can give. This is truth for every state of consciousness. It only means that if he petitions the Mahanta for a gift, he must have the state of consciousness for receiving it. If he does not, his petition is wasted. He cannot receive healing if he is not ready for it in his own consciousness. If he is desperate and grasping at straws, there is little opportunity for the fulfillment of his petition. If he seeks the Light before he is ready for It, expecting miracles, it is not likely that he will have the miracle. But if he seeks the Light and Sound and is in the state of preparation for It, then he shall receive the heavenly gift from the Mahanta.

The wretched, the poor, the unhappy, and those who are in need are drawn unto the Mahanta, for those who are poor in heart are the greatest recipients of his love. His weapons are love, the spiritual works of ECK, exhortations, and giving of himself.

He goes among the poor, the youth, the wretched, the wicked, and the unhappy to spread the Word of ECK. He gives only love, faith, and joy to all that he meets, whether it be an embrace, a kiss, a coin, or a coat. But to each he meets he gives all he has in spirit in the realm of the material world.

The Living ECK Master rejects all violence, all acts of force, and accepts his obligation to the society and order in which he lives. At the same time he refuses to obey any man-made law which interferes with his spiritual freedom and that of his chelas, which are the limitations put upon the body, heart, and Soul. The Living ECK Master recognizes the law of God.

The ECK is life and the Mahanta lives and creates life, for all things are made of ECK in accordance with the will of the SUGMAD. God took the ingredients of the ECK which are parts of the divine body of the SUGMAD, the shining dewdrops of the Ocean of Love and Mercy, and created Souls and life in which all nonbeings and beings live.

The true qualities of the Living ECK Master are indestructible. His chief quality of love can never be destroyed no matter what the enemies of ECK may do to him. Nor can any destroy his immortality. He may be put to suffering by men, caused pain and grief, but never can any bring about the true destruction of the reality of the Mahanta. He is permanent because he is perfected Soul, above the physical forms and physical substance. Never was he part of the perishable and impermanent. He is free from all that the ordinary man suffers, grieves over, and mourns in his losses and happiness in material gain.

The Living ECK Master is above time and space. He is God's essential expression and is never separated from the source of true wisdom and reality. He is able to see the past, know the future, and give healings, happiness, and create miracles for those whom he loves, and those who believe and can accept his gifts. For all those who have reached the state of consciousness of the knowing level shall realize who they are and shall be ready to receive the gifts as dispensed by the Living ECK Master.

The work of the Living ECK Master has already been finished with every chela who comes to him to be lifted up. He knows what the chela is ready to receive before the petition is made. He gives all to the chela in advance, but if the chela is not ready, there is no recognition that he has already received his gift. When the chela is ready, the gift shall be recognized and received with the joy and blessings of the Living ECK Master.

Those who are taken to the summit of the spiritual mountain by the Living ECK Master are the fortunate ones. Here, independent of time and space, above all the lower worlds, they see all the joy and blessings of life.

All reality stands out in its shining splendor and the Music of the heavenly ECK is acclaimed for all who have reached the summit. Below, the work of the divine ECK has already been done. It unfolds Souls who are in the lower worlds as long as each is within the tentacles of the Kal, and until each comes to realize It is living in the world of illusion.

Until then, each Soul exists in unreality. When the recognition of Itself comes in Self-Realization, It then will accompany the Living ECK Master into the heavenly worlds to find Its spiritual responsibilities in the worlds of God.

7

The Transcendence of Love

The major mistake that any chela can make with the Living ECK Master is to keep everything with himself in the personal realm.

This includes his own problems, and this is especially true of those who do not follow the path of ECK, yet will call upon the Mahanta to fulfill their petitions.

The question of love enters into the subject at hand. If the chela or the nonchela really loves the Living ECK Master, neither would make any petition for the fulfillment of personal desires through him. It is natural when one is desperate and has no other way out to make some contact through the physical channels available to ask the Living ECK Master for spiritual assistance.

It is not necessary, though. He should not have any demands made upon him through physical and material mediums but only via the inner channels. Therefore, if the pseudolove of any chela or nonchela tries to obligate the Living ECK Master by making extraordinary demands of him, there will be repercussions.

The Master should have the freedom to work in the universal cause of ECK. Instead, he has many people constantly demanding him to take care of any problem they may lay at his feet. These are the people who cannot accept love. If the Mahanta speaks a word of love to the chela, it must be taken in love by the one who accepts it.

The greater the following of the Mahanta, the greater will be the demands made upon him by those in ignorance. Few know that they are to take their own responsibility in life, for whatever they have is due to their own karmic patterns of life.

Those who profess love for the Living ECK Master must be sincere. If they are not, it is a useless gesture and useless words. Love does not come to those who seek it, but to those who give love. It is a binding force between Souls who have nothing to give but themselves to one another. It is not a physical force of any nature, but one of deep, tender compassion ready to give all should another demand it.

This love must be great for the Living ECK Master. If he should ask any chela to give up everything in life for the ECK, this should be done. Nothing should stand between him and the Master. Any opinions, any thoughts, any materialistic things, and any feelings should be given up to follow the Mahanta. Unless the chela is willing to do this, then he is not ready to enter into the spiritual worlds.

There are adversaries of ECK who will try to suppress the true spiritual works. Their behavior is abominable for they are not sensible, but panic and viciously attack ECK. Their attempt to repress ECK is damaging to themselves. Many pseudomasters will attempt to attack ECK and Its followers in order to stop the true message of Its reality. They cannot abide anyone who is not in agreement with their ideas and level of consciousness and who do not attempt to worship them as personalities.

This is proof that they have no love within themselves.

Those who follow these pseudomasters and abide by their words, mimic them in manner, and parrot their words against the ECK shall suffer. There is no proof of any spiritual development within these persons for they are only the agents of Kal.

It is wrong for anyone who makes claim to seership to publicly broadcast doom and disaster about an individual without that person's permission, or without first giving warning to that individual. This is a lack of love on the part of the so-called seer. This is proof that he is neither a seer nor a master.

Too many claiming seership have made their reputations in all times of human history by using others as their targets and victims. It has made for some a reputation in prophecy in a vicious, but Kalistic way.

The so-called prophets do not understand the laws of love, nor do they have any understanding of the laws of Kal that underlie all their statements. What they are doing is setting in motion, by public acclaim, some target for disaster, a series of vibrations which will eventually bring about troubles for their victims.

Such practices are always carried on in the psychic planes and have been during all recorded history. These peculiar persons create an aura of fear and awe, so they take advantage of it and strike down the foe and enemy with psychological effects made by fierce utterances and dreadful forewarnings.

If these pseudoprophets had any insight, it would be to their greater credit to serve their fellowman by quietly warning him, and breaking up the vibrations which are going to bring harm to him. Not doing so shows a lack of universal love on the part of these pseudoprophets.

Since these people are only looking for applause and acclaim, they manifest a great deal of their public utterances for public eyes and ears. This is only an ego builder, and they do more harm than good. They do not seem to understand that love for their fellowman is greater than their own petty egos.

The religionists of the world claim that when the whole human race comes to the path of love, all evil will disappear from the world. This is not a rational solution for few ever find the source of true love while living in the physical consciousness.

The fundamental requirements for meeting the Mahanta, the Living ECK Master are humility, love, and freedom from the bonds of any worldly religious creeds. Therefore, not many Souls will have the privilege of meeting the ECK Master. Moral goodness has nothing to do with meeting the Mahanta, nor do great intellectuals have any primary qualifications. It takes a Soul that has earned the right during Its past lives. All those who do come to the Living ECK Master have been with him in the past, not as the personality he now represents, but as Soul formed by the whole body of the ECK, the Word made flesh.

As one follows the path of ECK he will soon be assured that he is on the right road to God-Realization. He will become stimulated to greater love and charity for all. He will eventually be guided into the heavenly worlds where consciousness is blended into the divine Current, where Soul shall only see Light and hear only the Music of ECK.

The very heart of the doctrine of ECK is love. This love is that divine essence which unites all reality and brings together all Souls. The higher Soul goes into the other worlds the greater this becomes. Love is the bond which holds the worlds together. It is the living ECK, the Spirit of the SUGMAD.

When man turns his attention to universal love, all suffering ceases. This does not mean that all mankind at any given time in this world will collectively give

126

universal love. This is not in the consciousness of the human self.

If one begins to look for love, he will find it. If he puts any conditions on love, there will be obstacles. If he questions and argues with those who are the Arahatas, the teachers of ECK, over points in the spiritual works, he has not advanced on the path. None like to be told this but, nevertheless, it is true. Those who bring up points to be debated are still in the mental realm, and as long as they are there they will constantly have qualms and will debate love, freedom, and the meaning behind the words of the ECK books and those of the Living ECK Master.

He who is in this stage will search out the hidden meanings behind the Mahanta's words. He will seek significances where there are none. He will look for some reason for the Living ECK Master's acts. He will seek answers in everything but there will be none. He either accepts what is written in the holy works of ECK, or not at all. This is hard for those who have always been able to question and seek logical answers to all their questions.

The questioner, or seeker, must learn to control his curiosity. He must learn discipline, control of his thoughts, and to know whether his decisions and judgments are correct. He must settle down to some answers for himself which must be raised and answered within himself—not by the Mahanta, nor the Arahatas, but by himself. Then he knows without knowing. He understands without understanding and sees without seeing. He knows that whatever is said by the Mahanta is not of the physical temple worn by him, but of the ECK which flows through the embodiment. Whatever is written and whatever is said is not a symbol of any divine reason, purpose, or logic. But it is that which is from the original fountain of God and is not of any earthly origin.

127

Therefore, there is no significance to what is said or done, but IT is what IT is! Nothing more, nothing less.

The vital importance of love is to love all life without qualms, without wisdom or religion being uppermost in the mind of the lover. When one is of a pure heart and has the noble purpose of ECK as his goal, he can, impelled by love, set about doing the work of the SUGMAD on earth under the direction of the Mahanta.

Love is the keystone of the works of ECK. Without it no chela can enter into the heavenly kingdom. There is one direct command and that is to love one's fellowman and to love God more. Whosoever can measure up to this standard shall be ready for the Kingdom of God. But whosoever gains such love for the world can expect to gain nothing from the world itself. The Kal shall see that whosoever desires God while living in this world shall suffer for it.

Those who listen to the Mahanta and obey with love in their hearts shall find love everywhere. They shall receive the love of God and shall abide in the love of the Living ECK Master.

Those who love the Living ECK Master shall be loved by the SUGMAD. In love of this nature one finds freedom, but until one learns to love the Living ECK Master he is in the bonds of Kal.

No Living ECK Master ever works through a medium. He teaches that all wisdom is gained by changes in consciousness through contact with the ECK. Soul Travel is an individual experience, a realization of survival. It is an inner experience through which comes beauty and love of all life. It cannot be experienced in rituals and ceremonies, nor bottled in creeds.

The confusion in understanding ECK comes because every man's experience is different from every other man's. But the idea that man can get something from God because of his pettiness of human love is erroneous. This is not the kind of love which one should believe is true. Strength without love produces the brute. Love without strength produces the weakling.

The SUGMAD is love, wisdom, and power. IT is omnipresent, all-pervading. The Living ECK Master is the same, except that he has physical limitations. But spiritually he has complete freedom and is a replica of the SUGMAD. The body is not the ECK Master, it is only a covering, one of his ready instruments and the same as the Astral, Causal, and Mental bodies are only vehicles for him to use when on these different planes.

The Mahanta may instantly rise to those worlds above the planes of human and psychic activity where consciousness expands to limitless love, wisdom, and power. On return to this plane he has total recall of just as much of it as can be retained in the compass of the mental area. The Living ECK Master is infinite himself. If he has a hundred followers or one hundred thousand, it makes no difference. Each one will see the Living ECK Master in the inner chambers of his own individual self, wherever he may go. This, of course, must again depend upon the development of the chela's spiritual faculties.

The Living ECK Master always brings Light and Love into the world so that all men shall profit by them. Not just his own followers, but the world of itself. Each of those who follow him should be caught up in the fire of his love. This love begins in each like a tiny flame then begins to consume them until they love all because it is life, and life is God.

This is known as the holy fire. When the chela catches the spirit of the ECK, he immediately becomes fired to serve It. He is burning with the fever of the holy fire within himself, the ECK driving him on mercilessly toward fulfilling his destiny in this world. He becomes ruthless in his striving to get out the message to others and may be considered a missionary of the ECK.

This holy fire is a burning love for all things, all people, and all life. It is the love of God seen in the smallest blade of grass, or in the eyes of a newborn babe. It is the love of God stirring in Soul to find Itself, to give away everything which is holding It back materially in this physical world. It is ready to give up all the mental qualms, emotions, and attachments to anything in the material plane. It cannot help Itself, It is a babe in the power of the Lord. Everything but God is the anti-ECK, and It considers all as Its enemy unless it is part of what Soul knows as the ECK.

The holy fire of ECK is principally the love of God which has taken over the person who has surrendered himself to the Living ECK Master and found that this is the only path to complete liberation. The word *surrender* may be insufficient. It is not to be confused with its worldly connotation. It is that the chela fully trusts the Master in every department of his life. He trusts his spiritual interests in the hands of the Living ECK Master.

The chela never surrenders anything to the Mahanta which he must keep. It is merely that he puts his trust in the knowledge that the Master will take care of his spiritual guidance. He accepts the aid and guidance of the Living ECK Master over a path which is unknown to himself. The Master is the guide, for the chela starts out in a wilderness and must be carried out into the calm of the spiritual worlds.

But the Mahanta will never impose his own will upon any of his chelas. It is a cardinal principle that the Living ECK Master never interferes with the freedom of his followers. He is very careful of this for he seldom gives a command, merely advises, and never attempts to dominate the intelligence of others.

Complete surrender means that out of perfect confidence and a great love, the chela will gladly follow where the Living ECK Master leads him. By giving himself up to the Living ECK Master, in this sense, the chela gains everything, which ends in perfect liberty in the spiritual worlds. Yaubl Sacabi stated, "Give the ECK Master all that you have and he will give you all he possesses!"

Love, as it is known to human consciousness, is only involvement with astral influences. It is emotional freedom that one seeks; to be rid of this involvement of the astral influences. Until he can be rid of these he is never able to understand and know true liberation.

Human love which is involved with sentimentality and physical love is that part of the human consciousness influenced by the five Kal passions. These are: *kama*, or lust; *krodha*, or anger; *lobha*, or greed; *moha*, or attachment; and *ahankar*, or vanity. Of these man is influenced mainly by moha, or attachment. Here is the heart of man's karma, the very reason why he keeps moving constantly on the Wheel of the Eighty-Four, the continued round of births and deaths in this physical world.

This is the type of attachment which means delusive attachment, or infatuation. It is perhaps the most insidious of the five destructive passions. It is the one which makes the human consciousness believe that it can love all life; that it can love anyone outside itself. The truth of the matter is as Rebazar Tarzs once said, "He who believes that he has a great love for another, be it a fellow being or God ITSELF, usually loves himself more."

Once the human consciousness becomes absorbed in ECK, it has little time for anything else. The individual must decide whether he wants to be absorbed in himself or absorbed in God and the works of ECK as distributed via the Mahanta. Liberation of Soul is the one reason why man is in this world. Nothing else counts, but it is

131

the sole purpose of Kal Niranjan to keep Soul in this world, by using moha, the attachment to material things in life.

Kal Niranjan keeps men blinded to their own higher interest through the five passions. This particular passion, moha, or attachment, is the king of procrastination. It keeps the chela from attending to his spiritual interests, the Spiritual Exercises of ECK.

Should physical death come before man finds liberation, he will go through a period in the Astral world. He may be as asleep, or he may be aware of what has gone on around himself. But then he is given rebirth again into the Physical world, not remembering his sojourn on the Astral Plane, nor that he has lived past lives. He has not rested spiritually, and the Kal power takes him in hand again and leads him through the deep forests of worries and hardships of life.

He does this over and over again until one day he meets again with the Living ECK Master. This time he recognizes the Mahanta as the one he has been searching for all these many lives. It comes upon him like a burst of the sun from behind a cloud following a storm. Then he realizes what has happened to him and love for the Living ECK Master begins pouring out of him.

He realizes now that it is karma that binds the worlds of the lower planes together. The universality of the law of karma is one of the chief factors which binds life together, and not only human life but animal, plant, and mineral life as well. All these compose one big family, with a complicated and inseparable history and an inseparable karma. This is what man mistakes for love. It is not love but actually karma that binds him to all life here and on the psychic planes. He thinks of it as love because there is nothing within his mental capacity nor vocabulary that is capable of thoughts of love.

Then man begins to look at karma and wonders about it. When he comes under the great living Master he starts to realize that he has substituted love for attachment. This attachment is actually the karmic conditions of life that are holding him here. Once he gives up this attachment for life, he will begin to think in terms of a love which is a greater force than any other in this world or on the inner planes.

If man could possibly grasp the principles of karma, which he believes to be love, then there would be a complete change in the social structure of society in the physical worlds. He would then know that instead of having to pay off everything as a debt to the lords of karma, he would be able to take the way of Light and Sound through the ECK. He would know that in order to gain true love, all he would have to do is break his karma. This can be done by giving up his attachment to the things of the material worlds.

Man believes that peace comes through this lesser form of love. This is the great illusion of life, the works of the Kal power. Every man should know without prejudging that all life in this world pays for all it receives. There is no exception. If he does not give the highest love, without attachment, he is apt to pay for it somewhere in this world.

Every man must first seek to give love if he expects to receive it. He must give it under every circumstance— even though he is abused, mistreated, and given unnecessary hardships in this world. A demanding love is like a shadow for it has no substance. If anyone demands love in return for what he has not given, all is lost.

The cure for evil is the unobstructed Light and Sound. Evil is but a shadow, a lesser light and sound. It is nothing but the darkness which can become light through love. No one can ever come to the Mahanta except through the way of love.

When their good karma brings Souls into the presence of the Living ECK Master, it is because they have earned it. Their appearance may not indicate this good karma but, nevertheless, they have reached a place on the spiritual path which earns them the right. Their good karma was not utilized to bring them worldly position and wealth, but applied to secure for them something vastly more important. That is the Darshan, the meeting with the Living ECK Master. Few come with good bodies or prosperity, but with something far more important, and that is a capacity to love. This love is an inheritance that brings them to the Mahanta. They have but one idea and know nothing else, that the Living ECK Master will take them out of the misery and depths of this world. This is all that is needed. It does not require worldly goods of any nature, nor the need to have great knowledge. It is the good fortune of anyone who finds the Living ECK Master.

The Mahanta loves every Soul more than Soul loves Its defilements. This is truly the characteristic love of the ECK Master. If the Mahanta did not love his chelas more than they love themselves and their defilements, there would be little hope for any of them to ever reach heaven. This is the love of the Living ECK Master which surpasses all human understanding.

This is why the individual Soul must always go through tests while on the path of ECK. All the living Masters have gone through the same tests, have resisted temptation, have shown splendid loyalty to the SUGMAD and the highest characteristics of a Master. The chela who enters into this path must always maintain such an attitude in the presence of temptation and hardships. He must never weaken nor waver in his love or his loyalty to the SUGMAD and the Living ECK Master.

134

He who is fortunate to gain the attitude of true love shall have independence. Man must remain in this world as long as he has a single duty to perform, but he is not to love the world. He must not become so bound up with duties or family or worldly interests that he forgets his most important interests. He must never forget that one day he will leave friends and all possessions, and he never knows what day he shall be called upon to leave them.

Not only does he leave his own body. He can take nothing with him except his inner possessions. All material things and people belong to the passing show on earth, for they have only a temporary interest. These material possessions are not his own. They have never been, nor ever will be. They are the property of Kal Niranjan, the king of the negative worlds, and man's attachment to them is only temporary. He must never regard them as his own, but as a loan to him from Kal Niranjan for the day, the moment that he may both serve them and use them. When he comes to this attitude he has reached the *vairag.*

The wise never give thought for the dead, nor for the living in sentimental emotions. That which belongs to matter, heat and cold, pain and pleasure, and the values of beauty and ugliness, is impermanent. They come and they go and nothing shall halt them, for these are the elements of Kal, the negative power. The man who believes they are the core of his life shall suffer rebirth and death century after century until the day comes when he is able to cast the scales from his eyes and recognize the Living ECK Master. Then shall he see and know that the dweller of this world is vulnerable to the traps of Kal. Only Soul is free and cannot be forever held to the world of physical matter.

When one acts while dwelling in union with the Living ECK Master, and renounces attachments while remaining balanced evenly in spiritual and worldly successes and failures, then he has been liberated. This equilibrium is called ECKANKAR. Yet there is always compassion for one who works only for the fruits of his labor, who wishes to be rewarded for his deeds and actions in the physical life.

No man can reach God practicing any path except devotion to the SUGMAD through the Mahanta. One must be detached from all love of material things and events, from all concern about them. The chela attains this attitude—because his love is centered above the perishable things of this world—and reaches the heavenly planes.

From the love of objects of the senses man has desires; from his desires rises anger. From anger proceeds delusion, and from delusion comes confused memories and senses. This destroys his love of God, and from all this he perishes. But when he is disciplined and places his love in the Mahanta, then does he move among the objects of his senses free from pleasures and free from pain, but mostly free from self-indulgence.

Worldly peace can bring only the pain and unhappiness of life, for all peace is a momentary stilling of the senses which builds up a greater desire and bewilderment for the chela. He who detaches himself from the worldly peace of life shall achieve inner peace and shall be worthy of entering into the Kingdom of Heaven.

He shall have love for the things beyond the senses and shall hear the voice of the Lord speaking. Then shall he be devoted to life with the Word and form of the Mahanta in his heart, and shall attain supreme peace and an eternal home in heaven.

Only when one abandons his love of life, his love of material things and his anxieties, does he then begin to know God. Until then, he shall wander about the face of the earth life after life, incarnation after incarnation, un-

136

til that day when he shall meet with the Living ECK Master and see Truth as the many splendored love.

The three attributes derived from Soul's relationship with God are love, wisdom, and power. Of these three, the greatest is love. Man understands this more than he does the other attributes. Reality has but one attribute and that is love. All love is given to Soul when It is linked with the ECK, the Audible Lifestream.

One becomes the *bhakti*, the devotee, who loves all life more than he loves himself. He discards all rites and ceremonies and seeks to follow the Living ECK Master through the force of love only. When one reaches this stage of spiritual development he finds the Living ECK Master always in his inner vision, waiting to meet him at a point between the Sun Worlds and the Moon Worlds. This is the pure astral zone, where the lover of God enters a zone called the Ashta-dal-Kanwal. At this point the whole course of his life is changed.

It is the meeting with the Living ECK Master in his radiant body. This is the Mahanta's Nuri-Sarup, or Light form. It is the Living ECK Master appearing just as he does in his physical life, except that now his body is more beautiful and filled with a brilliantly illuminated light. The radiant ECK Master greets the chela with much love, and from there on the two are never separated throughout the journey to still higher regions and eventually to God. This inner form of the Mahanta is always with the chela from the moment of his initiation, but often the chela cannot see him. Yet from this moment on, the chela can see and communicate with the Living ECK Master on the inner planes as well as the outer ones.

There is no one else on earth but the Mahanta who can and will utter the Word which liberates the chela and puts an end to his uncertainty. He is the only one who can release Soul from Its prison, in this world. Otherwise there is no escape, for Soul is overwhelmed by the separateness of Itself from the universe of God.

This new stage in the life of the chela brings about a remarkable change in him. Up to this time his success has been partial. He has had the opportunity to test the exercises of ECK and repeat his individual mantra. From this moment on he may discontinue his chanting of the mantra for he will not need it. He is now in the presence of the Mahanta, the living Master, whom he may view constantly. This is the Dhyana, which inspires love for the Living ECK Master and the Master's love for him.

It is well in the beginning for the chela to understand that his greatest exercise is to look steadily at the Living ECK Master's form, particularly the eyes, be it in his inner vision or simply a picture of the Master. If one does this during his contemplation period, looking steadily into the eyes, he will find himself going into the other worlds more quickly than any other method. By softly chanting the Master's name and gazing steadily into his eyes he has the twofold essentials of the spiritual exercises, the Zikar and the Dhyana.

It is at this point that a great occurrence takes place. He will contact the ECK and Its perfect sounds will bring about changes within himself. He will find himself listening to that Music of the ECK within himself with increasing attraction and love. He will never want to leave It, or to miss one note of Its delightful strain. The chela who has reached this point will find that half of the preparation for his journey is done. While before he had to exert his willpower to focus the attention on the sounds of ECK, now it is difficult to withdraw the attention from It. The Living ECK Master and the ECK are attracting him, lifting him higher with each effort that he makes. He does not understand this, but it is his devotion and love pulling him ever higher with each step on the spiritual ladder.

He will have the most ardent wish to go on forever looking at the eyes of the Mahanta and listening to the Sounds of the ECK. One takes for granted before he starts on the path of ECK that he is to become well grounded in the fundamentals of righteousness. He must practice the Dharma, the law of life itself, in all aspects of his life. This means doing what one ought to do while an ECK chela. Without doing this he cannot make a start in life.

There is no pranayama in the practice of seeing the Mahanta during this Spiritual Exercise of ECK. The chela must sit in the proper position, with his mind detached from the world and fixed at the spot between the eyebrows, bringing all his attention to focus upon the singular eye. This has to be done if one is to go inside and behold the Mahanta. He softly chants the sacred name of God beholding the Mahanta with a loving gaze in the radiant form. The Zikar comes first and then comes the Dhyana, the vision of the radiant form of the Mahanta. Following this comes Bhajan, the spiritual exercise of listening to the Music of the ECK. No path to God has this form of exercise, mainly because none know the ECK Dhun, the Sound. They miss the most vital part of the realization of the SUGMAD in their lives.

This leads the seeker of God to the first experiences of Samadhi, to the actual going inside and stepping out onto the Astral Planes where he meets with the Mahanta in the Nuri Sarup. The highest form of Samadhi is the Nirvikalpa, in which the seeker of God cannot distinguish himself from the ECK Itself.

This is gained when the chela enters the Fifth Plane (the Soul region) with the Mahanta. It is here that he beholds himself as pure Soul after leaving behind his material sheaths. Few, if any, can attain this state without traveling the path of ECK in the company of the Mahanta.

No one can get his release from the net of karma without the Living ECK Master.

It is love that brings the chela to this spiritual stage in the heavenly worlds. It is love that makes civilization on this Earth Plane, and that love is the essence of pure Spirit. But the SUGMAD can never reveal ITSELF to anyone with a contaminated mind. The consciousness must be somewhat pure and ready for the ECK force to enter into it. Love makes this possible, and unless this quality is ingrained in man he must struggle until his consciousness becomes ready to accept it.

Adjustments to the discipline that the Mahanta suggests is the better way for the chela. It must be taken seriously and rigidly followed. This is what is known as the narrow way. One does not fit himself into this narrow way but he adjusts himself accordingly. He does the best he can without upsetting or disturbing his own way of life. Until he does this, time is wasted in trying to find himself and what the Mahanta is willing to do for him to assist him spiritually in this world.

Yet it is love, and this quality alone, which will gain him greater favor with God, and the Living ECK Master. Love and desire to serve make for a greater spiritual unfoldment on the path to the SUGMAD.

8

The Supreme Attainment of the Chela

The human body of the chela is Kal, the negative force. The body of the Living ECK Master is also Kal. Yet there is a difference between the two in their respective bodies. The body of the Mahanta is that of the ECK, the conscious creation. The body of the chela is that of his subconscious drives and desires from his past incarnations.

Both are made out of the elements of the Kal, which is maya. Each is then maya, but the Living ECK Master is conscious of it, and the chela is not. The Mahanta is the master of Kal-maya and the chela is its slave. The difference is the knowledge which is sacred and divine, and hidden from the sight of man.

Until the chela becomes an initiate in the works of ECK, he is unable to know and understand that he is the slave of Kal Niranjan. It is then that he begins to enter into the ECK, which is all-embracing and omnipresent, whether he is conscious of it or not. But when the chela raises the ECK from his subconscious potential state into full consciousness by opening the Spiritual Eye to Its Light, then only can Its nature become an active force in him and

141

free him from the deathly isolation of the Kal.

This is synonymous with the transformation of the mind and body into the state of Nirvikalpa, the highest state of enlightenment known as God-Realization.

Only in the state of Nirvikalpa can we realize the ECK as the body of the SUGMAD, that which we know as the ECK Itself. It is in this state that the chela can see the Mahanta as the personification of Truth. This is the state of suchness, the ultimate and unconditioned nature of all things of life.

One realizes this state by converting it into the ever present consciousness of the human state. Thus, he who is in this state finds himself in an all consuming focus of experience in which the elements of the little self are purified and integrated in the universal self.

The law which all seek to know is the great principle of life. Its simplicity is amazing for it is summed up in the statement: Soul exists because God loves It. In other words, all life exists because God so wills it. This is the very foundation of life, the whole of the philosophy of ECKANKAR. There is nothing more and nothing less. All life is built upon this basic principle of God. If Soul did not exist there would be no life anywhere on earth or on any of the planets, nor on the various and many planes throughout the universe of God.

If the chela could only grasp this very simple principle of life, he would have the entire philosophy of ECKANKAR in his hand. But so few can, because they cannot grasp the simplicity of it. They want to make it complex. This is why many fail in their search for the realization of the Almighty. Only when the transfiguration of body and mind has taken place does one enter into the understanding of the suchness of God, and the very heart of ITS being.

One must protect himself not only from without but

from within, and often from the most natural impulses. He must watch out, for Kal Niranjan will attack him from the Astral, Causal, and Mental planes as well as the Physical Plane. The attack that comes from these inner planes will be more subtle than he can imagine.

When he is first in harmony with the illuminated force It will increase like a violinist going up the E-string. He will believe that the Sound cannot go any higher and the Light will have to stop at what is considered the last point of its brilliancy. But the Sound will rise higher and higher, and God will bring the fortunate one from note to note like a deaf child being taught to hear or a blind child being taught to see.

Burning off of karma is the state of rechemicalization. It is something man must go through while living on this earth. Man should be able to do this under the Living ECK Master. If he is under any other guide here on earth, this is not likely to happen. He will be receiving more bad karma than good and will be overbalanced on the negative side. He needs to be balanced only in the middle way, not on either side. Only when he can walk the middle path of ECK can he leave the Wheel of the Eighty-Four and find the gates of heaven.

The Mahanta is always engaged in a dialogue with people, but his decisions and influence are constantly in a struggle with the opinions of man, which were formed by traditions and orthodox religious thoughts. Many men develop ideas on the rights and wrongs, the supposed motivations, the possibilities and impossibilities of each religious situation. Some of their ideas are well-based, some uninformed, some absurd.

The ECK which can be perceived by those who are not chelas is only a shadow of It. It takes on a different aspect according to the different viewpoints of the many planes of existence. Their crude perception of It does not in-

143

clude any concepts of Its possibilities for happiness and enjoyment. They see only glimpses of It in the works of the ECK around them.

Feeding the Kal force into the thought stream of this earth world builds an invisible body, a thought form, which is acceptable to all those who are susceptible. But those who allow the ECK to be fed into themselves shall do just the opposite, building an invisible force of love which shall protect, give life, and lift all they meet, see, or know into higher awareness.

God never reveals ITSELF to one who has an impure mind. Only when the stress of life has brought man to the verge of exhaustion, until the bruised body, the humiliated mind, or the weary self cries out for the Master will there come into his life the true Light. It is away from the applause of the crowd, the stage of life, and the wild cries of adoration that man finds himself confronted with the possibility of God. It is only in silence that he practices the Spiritual Exercises of ECK and finds the heavenly world. This is the underlying and absolute law; the essential message of the teachings of ECKANKAR. No one can find it in any other way.

It comes through the Living ECK Master, and until man comes to that stage of life when he must give up everything will he find all things necessary to his spiritual being.

Man is impressed by the remarks of worldly religionists that all truth is one and reality is the same for every man. This is not truth. Truth is a variation of experiences, and there cannot be any standard measure made of it. Those eternal truths which man speaks about so vainly and with such pompous pride are hardly more than mouthing words. He cannot prove what he says, nor can he debate them except from an intellectual viewpoint. Such statements are not truth. Anyone who experiences Truth knows it for what it is and has little to say about it. There are no words nor feelings which can express experience in the esoteric worlds.

The chela must seek love and wisdom before he attempts to have any experiences in the life beyond. He knows that if he surrenders himself to the greater cause of life, he will gain these attributes of God. But he also knows that if anything can save him from physical death—the transition of life from the matter world into the spiritual world—it is the Living ECK Master.

The Living ECK Master is always seeking the spiritually starved people of this world. He brings them more than bread. He feeds that spirit within them which is always urging them toward God. He is the ECK, the father, mother, and all things to all people. Where one may find him a friend, another will find him the Living ECK Master. Where one finds love in him another will find wisdom, and others may find hardly anything else but severe discipline. Each views the Mahanta from his own limited consciousness. He is all things to all people. Some will love him intensely, while others may dislike him with equal intensity. But no one will ignore him. He will be the target for attacks from all directions with every possible means that the Kal can invent, using the human consciousness.

Only the way beyond thought remains, the way of extended consciousness through Soul Travel. This way, or path, reaches far beyond the frontiers of primal thought into the realms of esoteric experience through the inner vision and spiritual sound of the ECK.

The language of words is replaced by the language of feeling, and the language of feeling is replaced by that of visual symbols. Then the language of visual symbols is replaced by that of sound symbols, in which the vibrations of Light and Sound are combined on a scale of

145

experience values until they become mentally exchangeable.

Should Soul cease to spiritually unfold It will, after the death of the body, go into the seven worlds of Avernus, the dark realm of the Astral Plane where many evil Souls must spend time. There is no purely evil man, nor is there a purely good man. However, many who border on the edge of evil, or who are tainted with some evil, must spend time in this dark world. Instead of extending himself into the higher worlds, he who has gained too much of the negative karma and overbalanced himself in this way must spend time in this vast world and later reincarnate into life again for the opportunity of regaining what has been lost in his spiritual unfoldment.

Once he has established himself and started working toward the good of existence, he will no longer spend time in these lower Astral Planes. After he has met the Living ECK Master and established himself upon the path of ECKANKAR, he will never have to reincarnate on this plane nor in any of the underworld planes. He will find himself ready for the heavenly worlds and will not return to the physical region again. He is assured of this by initiation into ECKANKAR.

Before one studies ECKANKAR the mountains are mountains and the oceans are oceans to him. However, if he should have an insight into ECK through the guidance of the Living ECK Master, then the mountains are no longer mountains and the oceans are no longer oceans. Later, when he has reached that state of God-Realization he will find the mountains are again mountains and the oceans are oceans. This, however, is a different state of consciousness, for now he recognizes them for what they are, nothing more. He puts no significance upon either the mountains nor the oceans for they are now a part of the reality of the matter worlds.

Where there is an understanding of spiritual love, there is neither concern with what life might be, nor care for the worldly life. Where there is an understanding of ECK there is no concern for searching for divine knowledge. Men believe that the body can be preserved with material foods alone. There are cases where the body is preserved but life does not exist, and yet man believes that he is alive. He is not alive until he is filled with the ECK. He is not living, nor does he have survival after the translation from the physical body, until he has been fed the food of the ECK by the Mahanta.

The wise man is one who stores up the ECK within himself and at the same time distributes the spiritual love which is within himself. He is not one who gives his compassion to a few but to all, whether or not many understand this. He is able to live among the wretched, the thieves, the unhappy, robbers and fools, for he accepts life for whatever it is and gives love to all. He is the wise one who is able to give all that he has to his fellowman. He finds love for those who greedily accept what he gives, and they shall be blessed a thousand times for his love.

Whosoever is beaten, whipped, scorned, mistreated, and derided while performing any of the works of ECK shall be blessed a thousand times over by the SUGMAD. He shall be freed of his karma and taken into the heavenly worlds where peace and joy shall be his eternally.

Whosoever shall suffer at the hands of the unbelievers while performing any works of the ECK, or in the giving of himself with love in the name of the Living ECK Master, shall be freed from the Wheel of Life and shall have no more worldly karma. He shall enter into the worlds of ECK (true spiritual worlds) and there live in peace, joy, and service as a Co-worker with the SUGMAD.

Blessed is he who shall give love in the name of the

Mahanta to any man or entity who does an injustice to him, regardless of whatever plane he may be dwelling upon at the time of the injustice. Whatever love the ECKist gives to another in the name of the Mahanta, he shall in turn receive love a thousandfold over.

Whosoever passes from his own physical body shall have heavenly awards if he whispers at the time of his passing the name of the Mahanta. He shall instantly be gathered up into the arms of the Mahanta and taken into the worlds of spiritual splendor. He shall never have to return to this universe of physical matter again. It matters little whether his length of time on the path of ECK has been two minutes or two hundred years; if he remembers the name of the Mahanta at the translation from his earthly life into the nether world, he shall be liberated and immediately initiated into the ECK.

Should he not be conscious at the time of his death, whoever is with him can perform the rites by whispering the name of the Mahanta, which impresses it upon the inner self and reaches the true being of the departing one. The same may be done for those who upon the last conscious moment of their earthly lives accept the Mahanta as their spiritual guide just before translation into the other worlds.

Many are called to the path of ECK, but few are ever chosen to become the true initiates of the nine worlds, and fewer still ever become eleventh world initiates. The highway into the Kingdom of Heaven is narrow, and the way is strewn with the spiritual corpses of those who have failed. Only those who give up all for the love of the Mahanta can ever reach the gates of paradise. This is not the heaven of the orthodox religionists, but the true world of the initiates who have earned their place in it.

He who listens to the Living ECK Master and obeys him will have his love and will be freed of his worldly karma. He will enter into the spiritual worlds a free Soul. If the living Master performs a miracle of healing, of bringing justice, or giving one something of a material nature, be not surprised for it is his nature to do such things when necessary. He will not perform miracles with fanfare, trumpets, or great pronouncements, but in silence and secrecy. He is the only one who can do such things. All others are false masters, false prophets, and false when they try to give and they have no means to give. No one but the Living ECK Master is the divine channel for these gifts of God.

Seek no favors from the Mahanta for he gives when he sees that gifts should be bestowed upon those who are in need. The seeker who is searching for some gift seldom has earned or needs it.

He who seeks to keep his life shall never have it. But whosoever loses his life in the love of the Mahanta shall have it in eternity. And whosoever shall give of his material life to the ECK shall have it thricefold returned unto him in spiritual blessings. No man with riches shall enter into the Kingdom of God, for he shall leave them on earth with his temple of flesh and both shall rot away into oblivion.

The chela must learn that in order to travel at will in the other worlds, he must first learn to break his covenant with the material worlds that are so solidly real to him. It is not a mark of power for one to travel in the inner worlds, but it is concerned with consciousness. This alone makes it possible for the chela to move at will on all higher planes of life.

There are an infinite number of planes within the universe of God. They blend and shift from one state to another. The vibrations are frequencies of which the ordinary man is not aware at any time. He believes that he is a body to which breath gives life with such an impact that it creates the impression that he is a physical body only. This is an illusion established by the Kal force which makes him human and limited.

The chela lives in a world of many mansions but he can learn to live on any plane. As he learns to break his agreement with this world, freedom will begin to come into his life. In time, he learns to accept the liberation which the Living ECK Master brings to him. He comes to control himself and not be controlled by matter or illusions. Anyone who is afraid of Kal Niranjan will never be able to control himself. He does not try to control or manipulate matter for this is useless. It scatters and disperses his energies to do anything outside of trying to control himself.

Those who speak of their Soul, or finding their Soul, are only working in the direction of the emotional (astral) nature. They do not mean Soul of Itself but of the emotional self, which is so often mistaken for Soul.

Hence, the Living ECK Master is the only one who truly knows what Soul is. He has taught since the beginning of time that one should never speak of Soul as "my Soul" or "his Soul." This is the negative connotation put upon It. He is the only one who can release Soul from these lower Astral Planes, the only one who can take Soul across the borders of death and bypass the Angel of Death.

Those who have borne their karma and do not look upon their own affliction with floods of unhappiness will be blessed by the Mahanta. Nothing is given and nothing is taken away. The Mahanta does not adjust the karma needed by the chela to develop spiritual responsibility. As the chela unfolds along the path of ECK he reaches the higher spiritual worlds where the Mahanta is ready to give of the divine gifts and take away what is not of any further use to the seeker of God. Thus one finds the illumination of the consciousness only through Soul Travel.

The matter world is but an extension of consciousness with a crust of solidity that must be broken. All the illusions of the Kal are but a part of material creation. This is fluid and bends to the creativeness of Soul. Those who retreat from life and do nothing are as bound in matter as are those who believe in the concept of a solid universe. Body and spirit are not separated from life but are a part of it as much as Soul. The nature of this world is change and impermanence.

It has been stated that the Living ECK Master can release Souls from the lower Astral Planes. This is also true of those who have reached the Ninth Plane of God under the Living ECK Master. These initiates of the Ninth Circle are privileged to name the Souls they want released, making it possible to unchain a dependent relative or anyone with whom they have close love ties.

Those who seek God shall never have the Light nor the Word. But he who does not seek God shall have ITS Voice which will guide him into the heavenly kingdom. The seeker does not like nor does he dislike, for there is only a hairbreadth difference between the spiritual kingdoms and those of the psychic regions.

A chela who wants Truth can never be for or against anything, for the grappling between acceptance and rejection is the failing of the ECK within one's consciousness and the delight of the Kal. One does not take and reject, nor does he drive away pain by pretending that it is not there. Pain will vanish, as all other problems will, by seeking serenity in the heavenly state. Whoever stops all movement in order to find rest only finds himself restless, and if he lingers over any extreme then he is both restless and lost.

In order to understand the Living ECK Master, stop talking, stop thinking, stop analyzing him and his worldly actions, and then you will understand all things. If the chela will look for the Light and Sound within the Living ECK Master, all things will be revealed to him.

The Mahanta is different from the outer form which the chela can see and talk with at all times. As the inner self, or the Inner Master, he is able to be in all places at the same time. He is the universal Spirit which is in all life and which manifests to every chela in the specific form that appears as the physical body of the Living ECK Master.

The chela has security when he is accepted by the Living ECK Master. He has gained liberation, salvation, and entered into the Kingdom of Heaven whether he is aware of it or not in his outer senses. He is now able to survive death. This victory over death is the greatest triumph of Soul. It is his privilege to have this knowledge and the grace of God bestowed upon him while living in this physical universe.

Those who seek God shall never have the Light or the Word for It can be gained only through the Living ECK Master. Those who look not for God shall have ITS voice, which shall guide them to the Living ECK Master who will lift them into the heavenly kingdom.

Every chela who wants to enter into the true realization of ECK truths shall and must become the extreme devotee of the SUGMAD. He must have the dominating faith that to serve the cause of ECK is the only purpose of his life. Only then will he succeed in becoming the ECKshar.

There is little need to seek truth, just stop having views. Do not adopt or reject, nor examine truth or pursue it. When the chela accepts the Living ECK Master for whatever he is, it is found there is no separation, no acceptance, no giving up of anything yet the surrendering of all he has within himself. Soul makes no distinction in any part of life. Therefore, there is no preference and attachments, thought nor disagreement, and, of course, no separation between the Mahanta and the chela.

Only the SUGMAD supports the universes. Those within the lower worlds are made up of the perishable, and those of the upper worlds are made up of the imperishable, the manifest and the unmanifest. Soul, forgetful of the Lord and of the fact that Its very existence depends upon the Divine Being, attaches Itself to pleasure and thereby is bound to the lower worlds. When It comes to the SUGMAD via the Living ECK Master, It is freed from Its fetters.

When the chela asks from whence do we come? Why do we live? Where shall we find peace, happiness, and rest in the end? What has command over my life to give me happiness or misery? Then the law of God states that "Soul has existence because God wills it." Thus, God loves all life so dearly that IT allows Soul to exist. If IT did not love life, there would be no life-forms in this universe and all would be barren. Time, space, law, chance, matter, primitive energy, and intelligence are only the effects of God's love for life, and only exist to serve Soul in Its journey to find liberation and freedom.

The Soul is not the cause for the law which brings happiness or misery. Not being free, neither does It act as the prime cause that brings about the opposite. As the free Self It has the opportunity to establish Itself as the prime mover for bringing about happiness and letting life be what it should be. It does not establish life but exists because life itself supports Soul as the prime consideration of God's love for every individual Soul within the universe.

The vast universe of the lower worlds is but a wheel. All beings and creatures existing within this universe are subject to birth, death, and rebirth. The one God, the

SUGMAD, exists only. All else is a part of ITS beingness. It alone presides over all. It dwells as the self-conscious power in all beings and creatures. ITS universe of the lower planes revolves like a gigantic wheel, and round and round go all beings and creatures until each meets with the Mahanta and finds the straight and narrow path of ECK.

As long as Soul believes It is separated from the ECK, It revolves upon the wheel in bondage to the laws of Kal Niranjan, which are birth, death, and rebirth. But when, through the grace of the Mahanta, It again realizes Its identity with him, It revolves no longer upon the wheel. It has found immortality.

Whosoever realizes himself as pure Soul knows that only by transcending the worlds of cause and effect through the Spiritual Exercises of ECK is one liberated. He learns that Soul is imperishable, that all within the lower planes is but the shadow of the true substance of the SUGMAD. Only the SUGMAD is the one Reality behind ALL. Only ITS body, the ECK, is what communicates to all ITS creatures. Only the Mahanta is the instrument of this communication, this Reality which flows out of the SUGMAD to all ITS beings, creatures, and worlds.

Thus, it is known that the Mahanta is that which is called the ECK in his spiritual body. He is the paradox of the worlds of God, for while serving in the Physical body in the lower worlds upon the material planes, he is also serving in the spiritual worlds in the Spirit body. As the ECK, the Spirit of the SUGMAD, he is able to be the whole and thus with all who recognize him as the Master. This is true, therefore, mainly of his own chelas. He manifests to his own as they can accept him.

As the ECK, the Mahanta becomes the all-pervading and omnipresent, transcending time and space, protecting those who are his beloved chelas and giving life to all that exists. He is the ECK, superior to all. Alone he stands; changeless, self-luminous, and living within the world yet not living in it. He is the Master, the ruler of the whole world, animate and inanimate.

Man's consciousness of Truth is the substance of his demonstration. To change his level of consciousness is the ECK chela's purpose under the Mahanta's guidance. Unless this is done there is little need for the chela to stay on the path of Light and Sound. It is not the gaining of knowledge but the understanding of Truth. Those who seek knowledge will learn that this is not the ultimate goal of the ECK chela.

Consciousness is the ECK, but not God ITSELF. The moment the chela has a consciousness of himself as the ECK, he has established himself in the Word, the Voice of God. This is the realization of Soul that occurs on the Fifth Plane. This leads into God-Realization, the ultimate goal of all chelas who follow the path of ECK.

Every Soul is the spiritual spark of God invested in a physical body. The body does not have to die for Soul to reach the spiritual universe during the time that It resides upon earth. Man does not have to become anything other than what he is in order to have divine guidance, divine protection, divine wisdom, and divine understanding through the Living ECK Master. He must recognize only that God is and that he himself, as Soul, also is.

Soul is never anything else but this. It is always in eternity. It is always in the present NOW. It is always in the heavenly state of God. These are the three principles of ECKANKAR which It must come to understand and know well. Out of these principles springs the doctrine and philosophy of ECK. There is nothing more to say and there is nothing less to say.

By the realization of these three principles the chela becomes a transparency for the divine impulse. He comes into a greater awareness of the divine plan in this world, and his part in it. He now rests in the arms of the Mahanta, the Inner ECK Master, and relies upon him to give him this divine guidance.

As he rises higher in this spiritual realization, the great discovery of life is found. The majestic law of God upon which the three principles of ECK rest is that "Soul exists because the SUGMAD wills it."

God loves all life so dearly that IT grants all Souls existence. IT gives life to all beings, entities, and forms. Without God's love there would be nothing—a void and a blank space in all worlds. Therefore, when the chela begins to understand this and know Truth, he has entered into the true worlds of God above the Atma Lok, the Soul Plane.

The SUGMAD gives of ITSELF, but IT also seeks that every Soul take up the path of ECK and find Its way back into the heavenly lok. But Soul must follow the narrow way as the SUGMAD wills and not as It desires.

9

Visions
of the SUGMAD

Within the visions of the SUGMAD are the followers of ECKANKAR who in some way or other
betray the Living ECK Master.

Many in their finite consciousness fail to recognize the
Master's true nature and thus cannot understand nor
control themselves in allowing their tongues and deeds
to react to the Mahanta and his words. Being in the flesh
they look upon him as man; but in Spirit, as the Living
ECK Master, he knows all that goes on within each of
the ECK chelas, although he never says anything. He
knows how each will end his life upon this earth, whether
he will stray from the path or will be critical, upset, and
unhappy with the Master; and whether he will betray
the Master during his sojourn as an ECK chela.

The Living ECK Master knows everything about the
chela as well as his reactions to the tests and trials given
him. The Master is never surprised when a chela leaves,
giving up in a quandary and unhappy because the
Mahanta has not given him the desires of his heart.
He knows the suffering that each chela may have
during these periods when separated from the

157

Living ECK Master.

The Mahanta is not concerned with what either the chela or the public thinks about him. He expects misunderstandings to arise or the masses to attack him, and he knows that some chelas, regardless of how much love is poured upon them, will betray him because of their lack of self-honesty. Those who quarrel with the principles of ECK, or the knowledge of whom and what the Living Master is to this world, had best examine themselves.

When one tries to correct the Master's works by suggestion or argument, he should take interest in what he is doing rather than accept these extremes. Often the Living ECK Master establishes certain forms of speech or written phrases which baffle the chela completely. But if the chela is open to what is being said, there is nothing which is perplexing. These are the tests of the ECK Master to see what the chela will take. If the chela accepts it for what it is, then the test is passed. It does not matter how the word is given as long as it is given out to the chelas.

The intellectual purist will never be able to advance on the path of ECKANKAR. He is so busy trying to find mistakes and errors in the sacred writings of ECK as well as others, that he overlooks what is necessary for his spiritual growth and defeats himself.

There are many ECK chelas who will complain and work up unhappy attitudes to compensate their egos. What they do not understand is that this is a destructive attitude and they are defeating themselves. The Mahanta will never speak out to them to correct this attitude but will quietly and without notice pull away from them. There is no way in which they can pull the Mahanta down to their level of consciousness. This is the very thing they wish to do.

It is self-defeating to deride the works of ECKANKAR,

to try to defy the spiritual influence of the ECK or look upon the SUGMAD and the Living ECK Master negatively, or with the eyes of Kal. The ECK Master has always been a figure of controversy in the materialistic world and will always be, for he is a spiritual giant in the flesh. He could bring peace and happiness to this world, but it is not his purpose. The races and people of the earth are willing agents of the Kal power. They perform his duties to keep any spiritual influence out of this materialistic world, including that of the Living ECK Master if at all possible.

The mission of every Living ECK Master is to find those who have a deep desire to prepare for returning to their true spiritual home, the Ocean of Love and Mercy where they will become a co-worker with God to prepare as many as possible during their earthly lifetime to become a channel, an instrument, for the divine power. This will give them the opportunity to be able to assist the Living ECK Master in his work and to lift others in spirit, to help him prepare them for their ascent into the Ocean of Love and Mercy.

Since it is the mind which creates the human body and controls it, it follows that the more it reflects and is filled with the body of the ECK, the more it will be able to influence and transform the physical body. This transformation brings about perfection in greater abundance in daily living. Not the abundance of materialistic life but in the fulfillment of Spirit. It gives perfection in Spirit and in love for the chela who is able to reflect this to all with whom he comes in contact.

When the chela reaches this vastly important state of transformation, he is able to see the illusory body (often called the phantom body, a concept of the physical body which is as misleading as the maya-illusion belief). Many define this world as maya, but the ECK chela should not think that the world is deprived of all reality—only that it is not what it appears to us. Its reality is only relative. It represents a reality of a lesser degree which, when compared with the highest reality, the Ocean of Love and Mercy, has no more existence than the objects of a dream or a cloud formation. Only the ECK Masters, the perfectly enlightened ones, have access to these higher worlds to make such comparisons.

Bodies are the expressions of an inherent law whose reality is undeniable, even though they are products of the Universal Mind Power, known as the Kal force. Though the body and mind are products of these worlds, and the individual personality is both mind-made and illusory, it does not mean that they are unreal. The mind that creates them has made them real in this world, for they are necessary for Soul to use as an instrument while here.

The body and personality do not disappear the moment we become aware of either as products of the mind, nor when we become tired of either. As soon as these products of the mind take material shape they must obey the laws of matter, energy, space, and time. No Master, regardless of his degree of spiritual unfoldment, can arbitrarily change or annihilate the material properties and functions of the body. He can only transform them step-by-step, by controlling them in their initial individual states until he has reached a certain level of spiritual perfection.

The Living ECK Master reaches this state in time to take over his position as the spiritual emissary of his times. He is not restrained to any particular place. The ECK Masters who have received the Rod of Power only relate to those in this world who will listen to the true path and to those who come seeking true knowledge.

The ECK Masters are not linked with any orthodox religious cause or dress. They are free personalities, for they are neither a party to one nor a foe to the other. They only impart knowledge of the way to reach God. Those who apply themselves to the path of ECKANKAR will succeed, and those who keep themselves aloof and far away from ECK will not succeed to the higher levels of the spiritual worlds.

The mission of true spirituality can only be carried on successfully by the Living ECK Master. It cannot be entrusted to those who have not reached the worlds above the Atma Lok. Whosoever attempts to reach God can only go through the Mahanta and not through those who are seeking the possession of the world. Be not deceived by such people. Do the Spiritual Exercises of ECK and meet the Mahanta in the other worlds.

To be with the Mahanta inwardly and enjoy his talk, his blessings—to see the ECK power working in the mortal coil—is an ultimate experience. The Living ECK Master's connection with his chelas is eternal, unshakeable, and loving. He desires to see all chelas rise to spiritual heights and continually pours his love, protection, and grace upon them, making them more receptive to the ECK.

The understanding of survival in the higher spiritual states of existence is linked with certain esoteric experiences, which are so basic in nature that they can neither be explained nor described. They are so subtle there is nothing to which they can be compared; nothing to which thought or imagination can cling. Yet such experiences are more real than anything else in this physical world. More real than anything that the senses of the human consciousness can experience, touch, taste, hear, or smell because they are concerned with that which precedes and includes all other sensations; and mainly because reason, logic, and intellect cannot be identified with any of them.

The ECK follower knows that it is only by the means

of symbols that such experiences may be somewhat expressed to the world. These symbols can only be hinted at and are not invented. They are spontaneous expressions which break through the deepest regions of the inner self and are brought forth outwardly.

The forms of divine life in the universe break forth from the seer as vision, from the mystic as Light, and in the ECK initiates up to the Fourth Circle as Sound. But the Mahdis, the Initiates of the Fifth Circle, have vision, Light, and Sound. The higher each goes on the planes of the worlds of true Spirit, the greater the vision, Light, and Sound become.

Therefore, the chela now understands that sounds coming from the mouth of the Living ECK Master are not ordinary words but the true Word, the mantra, the ability to create an image in its pure essence. All that he says becomes knowledge, the truth of being which is beyond right and wrong; it is real being beyond thinking and reflecting. It is the ECK force speaking through the Living ECK Master. It is beyond true contemplation as every Mahdis, the Initiate of the Fifth Circle, will come to know. It is the simultaneous awareness of the knower and the known.

A personal mantra, the secret word which fits each initiate, is an instrument for linking up with the ECK. With its sound it brings forth its content into a state of immediate reality. The Word is the ECK power, not merely speech. The mind can neither evade nor contradict it and will often wrestle to keep from accepting it. But whatever the Word expresses, by its very sound it exists—and will come to pass in each of those who use it. The Word is action, a deed immediately calling forth reality. It is not merely a sound, but an action of the ECK in motion upon whatever plane the initiate is performing.

The secret of the hidden power of the ECK—sound or

162

vibration—forms the key to the riddle of the universe and creativeness. It reveals the nature of God and the phenomena of life understood by the ECK Masters throughout the ages. The very sounds of the vibrating form a universal harmony in each element throughout the whole world.

The knowledge of the creative Word lives deeply within the heart of every ECK initiate. Each learns early in his study of the spiritual works of ECKANKAR for It is the very heart of all life. He who has the true knowledge knows that in the lower worlds there exist both creative sounds and destructive sounds, and that he who can produce both can, at will, create or destroy. But only the Living ECK Master has this power for it is given to him who will sustain life for all.

The holy ECK, or the Word, must be practiced in silence. Only those who have received the Word in initiation can be given the blessings of the SUGMAD through the Mahanta. The practice of the personal secret word of each initiate shall be done vocally when alone or silently while in public. He shall practice not only the Kamit, the law of silence, with his secret word but shall practice the silence in his own affairs with ECK, and whatever is given him in the secret teachings.

Whatever the Mahanta, the Inner Master, gives him in secret through the channels of the inward self, he shall keep secret and not speak of to anyone else. He shall practice this law of silence with others who are not to be told any of the deep secrets of ECK. He will not speak about the Mahanta and their inner relationships, nor of his affairs in the works of ECKANKAR. Those who do are violating the very heart of the works and shall have to pay in some manner or other.

One may discuss the outer works of ECK with those who are interested and seeking spiritual security. He may discuss the outer works for those who want to learn more in order to take up ECK as a chela and follow the pure path into the heavenly world. However, one shall never give openly the esoteric or the secret works of ECK, especially those who have become initiates in ECKANKAR.

Every chela will at some time or other be confronted with the riddle of faith. Each will in turn be attacked by the Kal in some manner or other because of his relationship with the ECK. This faith will be tested by the pseudomasters and the false prophets. Many will speak to the chelas, in the name of another religion, as a master, or what they call the true faith. Some will speak in the name of the Mahanta and ECK Master. But they speak with false tongues for none but the Living ECK Master has the authority to speak in the name of the SUGMAD.

Anyone, from a king to a barber, who wishes to listen to the teachings of ECK from the Mahanta, follow him in his missionary wanderings, or join the ECK Satsang (the formal fellowship of ECK disciples) is free to do so. But in all, the original transgression in ECK is ignorance. This is not merely an absence of knowledge, but the wrongness of attitude. The approach of the ECKist to God is through the Mahanta, with the attitude of separation of Soul free from the lower selves.

Soul must be freed of all skandhas. These are ideas, wishes, dreams, and consciousness of the lower self which creates attachments to the physical realm. When Soul approaches God with only love to give, then It is accepted into the heavenly realm. All the riches and wealth of the earth and its companion planets cannot get a single Soul into the heavenly worlds. The way is love, nothing else. This is the only path an ECKist travels.

Love comes through the practice of the Kamit which is the law of silence. No one can enter into the state of love until he knows loyalty, devotion, and love for the

ECK. Until he surrenders to the Mahanta, giving up everything to gain love, his life shall be narrow and selfish. His loyalty, faith, and devotion are his survival factors, both in the world of human consciousness and the worlds of the psychic senses. No physical survival factors are concerned when the body is destroyed through accident, bullets, or disease. But much can be accomplished in saving the body and repairing it if disease or war brings injury to it, and it can safely pass from the cradle to death without any harm or injury. Yet many men are taken away due to such factors as stupidity, mental instability, and lack of faith, devotion, and loyalty to the ECK.

The initiates, mainly of the Fifth Circle, do not suffer from insanity, instability, neurosis, or worry. They can stand up under the sufferings which the Kal force tries to inflict upon them. Resistance to disease, accidents, and other poor physical survival factors are common to these spiritual ECK initiates. The higher one goes in the initiations the greater become his survival factors, both in the psychic and the spiritual worlds.

It is quite wrong to think there is no personal self, that is, a human consciousness. When one rises above the human consciousness and its states of mind passions, then It dwells in the spiritual states. But Soul is never without having to live within the human consciousness as long as It has a physical body and must dwell in this world. This means that survival is in the Soul state and not in the human consciousness.

The chela does not annihilate the human self but takes it as part of the whole being until it is eliminated by physical death. He must never leave the physical body while the body is still alive and try to stay in the other worlds permanently. He must learn to live in the two worlds at the same time, knowing that the death wish is

165

only in the human consciousness and never in the spiritual self.

The death wish is instilled in the human consciousness. It is there when one feels that nothing gives happiness and, therefore, it is impossible to ever meet with any spiritual success. Those living in the human consciousness will seek happiness through orthodox means which the old religions and philosophies of the world teach. Neither are of any value to the chela who wants to get into the heavenly kingdom.

Orthodox religions represent the human and astral states of consciousness, while worldly philosophies are concerned only with the intellectual or the Mental Plane. All these are only of the psychic world and give only the teachings of these planes which are under the Kal Niranjan. It is his desire that all who live in the human body have the wish of self-destruction implanted within them. This keeps Soul trapped in the lower worlds under his rule. It is his duty to see that all Souls are kept here. Therefore he must resist the ECK from taking them out of his domain.

It is also his duty to see that man is filled with woes and miseries. It is part of his plan to see to it that as many as possible in the human state of consciousness hinder the work of the Living ECK Master and all those who follow him in the lower worlds. This is the way the Kal works, although he has little success when he attempts to interfere with the Living ECK Master and his mission.

The Kal encourages suicides, self-destruction, unhappiness, apathy, discontent, disruption of communities, and complaints. He encourages lust, anger, greed, attachment to material things, vanity, abnormal sex activity, craving for drugs, alcohol, tobacco, gluttony, gossip, obscene literature, useless card games, laziness, thinking

166

ill of others, taking offense easily, criticizing the actions of others, lecturing on mistakes of others, chronic fault-finding, scolding, nagging or blaming others for things that go wrong, vile abuse, cursing others, fighting, quarreling, or trying to inflict injury on others.

He also encourages miserliness, hypocrisy, perjury, misrepresentation, robbery, bribery, trickery, bigotry, self-assertion, a show of wealth and power, gaudiness in dress, and the exhibition of a domineering attitude. He dearly loves titles, honors, degrees, procrastination, worry and anxieties, divorce, controlling others, mob actions, deception, ridicule, resentment, murder, tyranny, boasting, and exaggeration. Kal assumes great intellectual knowledge, long and unnecessary periods of meditation, shabby beards and hair, and untidy dress.

These are among the many things which the Kal power will try to encourage in any chela. It will even try to bring about a break between the chela and the Mahanta. It will create all sorts of doubt in the chela's mind as to what the Mahanta is doing and why it is being done. It will bring about an estrangement between the ECK Master and the chela. But at no time will the Living ECK Master ever be disturbed at such foolishness for he can see through the illusions which the Kal establishes for anyone who falls into such traps.

The chela who allows himself to be persuaded by the Kal power is only adding to his karma. He should not let himself fall into slovenliness of appearance or mind. This adds to the karma of whoever does it. He should know that any of these patterns of physical, psychic, and other lower plane habits are only karmic in nature and often considered overt acts against others.

Those who fail to give dignity and respect to their neighbors, elders, and loved ones will have to suffer the consequences. Those who fail to love and try to understand the Mahanta are placed in a long series of incarnations until they come to this state in some future life.

All the works of ECK, therefore, are based upon three tenets. First, the works of ECK form a nucleus for the universality of life through the spiritual hierarchy of the ECK Masters. Second, they promote an opportunity for all those who desire to earn their way past all karmic burdens and enter into heaven for eternity on passing from this lifetime through death. Third, they will prove to all persons that survival throughout eternity is possible through experiences under the guidance of the Living ECK Master, here and now.

Therefore, one has to think about life as being just IT. There are no disclosures given in what are called the right views or understanding: right purpose or aspiration, right speech, right conduct, right vocation, right effort, such as the Buddhists give. What the chela is seeking is simply one thing. This is the Truth, and once this happens he will find that nothing else matters. The eight steps of Buddhism are concerned with the mental regions which have always been under the control of the Kal forces. Therefore, the ECK chela cannot afford to put his mind on the lower elements but must at all times receive the guidance of the Living ECK Master who eventually will separate knowledge from Truth for him and show him the gap between them.

Knowledge lies in the lower worlds. It is the bane of the seeker after God, and no chela has much interest in this quality of the psychic world. Of course, it is of immense value in the lower world kingdom, but at the same time it has little value in the true spiritual worlds. Most chelas will go through this phase of unfoldment and think of titles and knowledge as the ultimate. But this is wrong as neither have anything to do with the true value of life. One chela who is completely ignorant of any academic knowledge and psychic erudition or wisdom can be great in divine wisdom because of his ability to contact the world of God.

He knows without having gone into the art of study. This knowing holds a strange quality that no wisdom of life in the lower worlds can furnish. It is something that reaches out and tries to touch each individual, if such Souls have readied themselves for it. It will make no effort to enter the consciousness of the individual unless that Soul is ready and willing to accept the higher understanding of life. Thus it is said that the ECK only accepts those who are willing and ready for Its divine gifts.

The insistence in ECK on the proper use of will and mind in the lower worlds is part of the need for living in both the physical and spiritual realms at the same time. The psychic world was purposely left out because it is the mental area and included in what is termed the physical and spiritual realms. Actually, the chela lives in three worlds: the human consciousness, psychic consciousness, and the spiritual consciousness simultaneously and singularly.

This is the explanation of Soul Travel, but too many think of it in terms of phenomena. It is not psychic phenomena, but that one can inwardly see the Living ECK Master and hear him talk; can see him walking on the street through the inner eyes and can hear him talking with the inner ears. One can visit the worlds beyond the physical body with the Mahanta, the Living ECK Master through this inner vision. It is inner travel; the moving of one's consciousness from one state to another.

When the chela's spiritual eyes are open he sees the Living ECK Master, talks with him in the nonverbal tongue and listens to the secret teachings with nonphysical ears. Many are not able to do this because they do not believe; others cannot do this because they allow their little selves

169

to get in the way; another group cannot do it because they are depending on psychic phenomena, and if they have no abilities in this field they will fail completely.

When one contacts the Living ECK Master in the other worlds, he is doing it personally. It is not something psychic but something deeply spiritual. It is beyond conception or understanding. It is Soul movement from one plane to another, not the movement of the various bodies of man, which is dangerous.

No entity can take possession of anyone's body when he is Soul Traveling. He has no need of the silver cord for it is dropped when he enters the Atma Plane (Soul region) and picked up again when he descends to the body. He gathers up the profound teachings of ECK as he moves about the realms of the upper worlds, the true universes of God.

Those who need the Living ECK Master will always stay with him, but those who feel that they are beyond this are wrong in their thinking. They have not examined the truth, and will go afoul of the illusions established by the Kal. They will find that nothing can revive them except the fresh spirit of ECK, the winds from heaven. They cannot hear the true melody of the ECK, nor hear the Living ECK Master's words inwardly or outwardly. They can neither understand nor grasp the true nature of the works of ECK. Neither can they find the Mahanta within them at all times. They will see him occasionally and have a revival of faith but then it will leave because this is impermanent.

To have permanency the chela must have faith and live in the presence of the Living ECK Master, whether or not he can see him with the inner eyes or hear him with the spiritual ears. It is always true that the Living ECK Master never leaves anyone with whom he has established his love. He gives of himself and does not neglect the chela and his affairs.

The secret word which the initiate receives during the initiations of the different circles (planes) is not merely sounds to be repeated to one's self, but powerful expressions of the ECK power. Such words do not act of themselves but through the inner self which experiences them. They do not have any power of their own; they are only the means of concentrating already existing forces. They are like a magnifying glass; it contains no heat of its own but concentrates the rays of the sun. It transforms these rays from a mild warmth into a burning heat. The same applies to the secret word of the initiate. His word transforms him from the confused doubtful seeker into the incandescent lover of God.

Those who confuse the hidden knowledge of their personal word are like the primitives who believe in sorcery. Scholars who try to discover the nature of these words with their philological knowledge often come to the conclusion that such words are meaningless. Yet it is known that those who have received a personal secret word in their ECK initiation have gained in their unfoldment. This is a tradition among the followers of ECK over the past centuries that has proven to be an expression of the deepest knowledge and experience in the realm of spiritual life.

Those who have received a personal secret word from the Mahanta, whether it is through one of the Mahdis (initiates of the Fifth Circle or above, who can give the initiations), or from the Mahanta in person (outwardly or inwardly), shall never reveal their word to another without permission. It brings the spiritual unfoldment of the chela to a halt. He will not have any more advancement until given another secret mantra to replace the other.

The philosophy of the secret teachings is built around

171

this phase of ECKANKAR. In ancient times the ECK Masters, as members of the Order of the Vairagi, taught orally and inwardly. The teachings were rarely, if ever, put in writing. The teachings were therefore given mainly in the inner sanctum, meaning that all were given individually to the chelas through the inner channels.

This meant then that the chelas were chosen by the Mahanta, as they are today. Every Living ECK Master chooses his chelas and few are let go. If they do wish to go, it means they leave voluntarily and it is mutually agreed upon. If a chela decides to leave the Living ECK Master on his own without first discussing it, then he has problems to face which are more severe than ever. He has left the ECK Master and gone into the wilderness alone to face the wild beasts which will devour him. It is typical of the vain chela to announce that he is leaving without asking permission.

No chela who has asked permission to leave the Master's care has been refused, for the Mahanta gives him freedom to do as he wishes. He does not warn him against the dangers that the chela will face after leaving the protection of the Master. Neither will the Living ECK Master refuse to take him back should the chela wish to return to the fold of ECKANKAR.

If a chela decides to leave the Living ECK Master, the Master will not punish nor will he give any indication of what might happen to the chela. This is for the chela to learn on his own, for the experiences he meets are his own. It is when the chela leaves the protection and guidance of the Living ECK Master that Kal Niranjan will pounce upon him and start his negative works.

The specific qualifications for the initiate are: a basic knowledge of the main tenets of the sacred scriptures of ECKANKAR, a readiness to devote a certain number of years to the study of the spiritual works of ECK, and

172

practice of the inner teachings under the guidance of the Living ECK Master. Thus the initiate will find that the esoteric knowledge is open to all who are willing to exert themselves sincerely and who have the capacity to learn with an open mind.

Just as those who are admitted for higher education in academic institutions in this world must have the necessary gifts and qualifications, so have the Living ECK Masters of all times also demanded certain qualifications from their followers before they initiated them into the inner teachings of ECK. Nothing is more dangerous than half-knowledge, or knowledge which has only theoretical value. This is why the SUGMAD has placed within the worlds a living representative of ITSELF.

The experiences of Soul in realization of Itself and Its mission can only be acquired under the guidance of the Living ECK Master and by constant practice. After such preparation, the individual secret word is used and all the accumulated forces of Its incarnations are aroused in the initiate. This produces the conditions and power for which the word is intended. The uninitiated may utter any specific word or mantra as often as he likes, but it will not produce anything for him.

The secret of the special individual word for each initiate is something not intentionally hidden. But it has been acquired by self-discipline, concentration, inner experience, and insight. Like everything of value and every form of spiritual knowledge, it cannot be gained without effort. In this sense it is like profound wisdom that does not reveal itself at first glance because it is not a matter of surface knowledge, but a deep realization of the inner self.

This is also true of divine love. One does not see and grasp it at first glance but it grows within him like the acorn of the oak in the earth. Gradually it opens the consciousness of the receiver and flows through to the world, changing all about it.

10

The Purpose
of the Kal Power

The SUGMAD's purpose in establishing the Kal worlds is to train each Soul to reach the perfection of being a Mahdis, an initiate of the Fifth Circle, which is being a Co-worker with the Mahanta, the Living ECK Master.

It is the purpose of the Kal power to temper each Soul in the art of life so that It can come to the Mahanta as a chela. Hence, he initiates every chela who can become qualified after two years of study on the path of ECKANKAR. He wants every chela who is eligible to become an Initiate of the Fifth Circle.

Therefore, Kal Niranjan was created and is subject to the laws of the SUGMAD. His duty is to create hardships, illusions, and make the path of life more difficult for each Soul who must travel through the lower worlds trying to reach God. These illusions are to make Soul believe that nothing exists beyond this world. But all in all, the SUGMAD intends these lower worlds of Kal to be the school of life which all Souls must attend before moving on to the heavenly path of ECK.

Until the lesson is learned that these worlds are only

regions of illusion, none will meet the Living ECK Master. One will struggle forever upon the path until the day it dawns on him that all the glories and wealth of these worlds are merely the toys and playthings of Kal Niranjan. Then will he find the Mahanta awaiting him.

The Mahanta is the key to all things for the chela in ECK. He is the great Soul, free from the illusions of the Universal Mind worlds under the rule of Kal Niranjan. He is the only link between man and God and, therefore, it behooves all to enter into the path of ECK to find their way to the SUGMAD with the assistance of the Mahanta. He is the linkup with the divine Deity and is able to give the initiation that puts the chela in true contact with God.

The Mahanta is not a citizen of any country, although he will physically live in one and obey its laws. But he is a citizen of the whole universe of God and is known as a man of God. He is the universal man who is here to give the chela the right way to God and nothing else. When anyone appeals to him for material help it depends on whether or not the Mahanta believes it is best to give it. If he believes that it is needed, then it will be done. But if it is a hindrance to their karma and their spiritual unfoldment, it shall not be done.

He who hates the Mahanta will hate God, and he who loves the Mahanta will love God. This is what is known as the cell of self-cognition, for man of himself can do nothing. It depends mainly upon God working through the great instrument of ITSELF, the Mahanta, whose several bodies act as channels for the ECK power on every plane throughout the universes of God.

However, the key to the survival of ECKANKAR in this world is the Mahanta working with the Mahdis, the Initiates of the Fifth Circle and above, who are his chief channels for the ECK power. It also means that the ECK Satsang is equally important to the survival of ECK in

176

this world and upon every plane of the spiritual universe.

The Mahanta not only works in this world as a true channel for God, but upon every plane of the spiritual worlds. The Mahdis, therefore, are able to work only in this world and in the first five planes as distributors of the ECK power. But they are only qualified to do this by the love of the Mahanta, who allows each to be a channel for himself and the power that flows through him. There is no other way to be linked up to God except through this method.

Therefore, ECK and Its message are distributed through the Mahanta to each of the Mahdis for every plane in the lower worlds; the Physical, Astral, Causal, Mental, and Etheric. Each Mahdis depends upon the Mahanta for this, and acts as a channel only because he allows it. Also, there must be ECK Satsangs, not only in this world but upon each of the lower planes, for each acts as a collective channel for the distribution of ECK power.

So long as the ECK controls the ECK Satsangs, It is in the position to give life to the individual and the Satsang, respectively. This is the reason for Its longevity in this world, for It cannot be destroyed. Defeat or the dropping out of an ECK Satsang does not dissolve It or even make an impression.

The heartbeat of ECK is faith in the SUGMAD and the Mahanta, whether the chela belongs to an ECK Satsang or performs upon his own, while the believers in orthodox religions put their faith unwittingly in Kal Niranjan. This type of faith is only an opinion, fixed in the minds of men. When all the relatives and absolutes of any Kal-directed group are brushed aside, the individual finds himself alone. This is not true of those chelas who follow the ECK, for the ECKist knows that the presence of the Living ECK Master is always with him. He is never alone.

Moralistic power is the only force by which Kal

177

Niranjan can operate. The Kal has no other force in this world than what we call the forces of nature. But moralistic power works best in man because of the consciousness of human nature. Man lives by this moralistic power which builds churches, civilizations, and societies; he makes laws and enforces laws through it.

The ECK power is above the dichotomy of good and evil, for It is only the power of the true nature of the SUGMAD. It cannot be otherwise. It leads Soul back to heaven; It has no other purpose. The true purpose of the Kal, however, is to hold Soul within the lower worlds, torment It, bring It hardships, and build Its life in the depths of negativism through centuries of incarnations.

Within this true physical realm, Kal Niranjan works through the human consciousness. The Kal force performs best in the political and religious arenas, for here it is working through the absolute rule of a single body of consciousness, or that of a single individual.

No matter how the system of representation, or delegation, of the orthodox religious system is arranged, there is necessarily an alienation of the liberty and freedom of individual Souls. All religions use bodies, minds, and Souls, for without exception the ways they seek for power are varieties of absolutism.

This is true especially of the worldly religions. These systems fail to recognize that though man is a social being and seeks equality, he also loves independence and freedom.

The desire for personal property, in fact, springs from man's desire to free himself from the slavery of tribal or state-owned beingness, the primitive form of society. But property, in its turn, can go to the other extreme. It can violate equality and support the acquisition of power by the privileged minority who are generally behind the religious systems of the earth and other worlds.

Each chela in ECKANKAR must listen to the voice of the Living ECK Master, for he is the speaker of the Word of the SUGMAD. Each ECKist will eventually become an Initiate of the Fifth Circle (plane). He is then a citizen of the Fifth World and must perform all his living acts within this new universe. Thus the fifth dimension is where he begins to live truly in the spiritual Light and Word.

It is no mishap that he reaches this state of spiritual unfoldment. He then becomes the agent of the Mahanta, and he has the ability to work in silence, but at the same time openly, as Co-worker with the Mahanta. But he himself always has to confront the Kal power, for it will assault him again and again, each time trying to create doubt, trying to break through to create schisms and bring about unhappiness with the spiritual works of ECK.

The works of ECKANKAR are revolutionary and eternal. The ECK changes all things once It is allowed to enter into the consciousness of the individual who is earning his daily living. No matter what the situation may be or what that individual does, and regardless of his position on the social and economic scale of society, he has become a channel for the ECK to change the environment within his own world.

The Living ECK Master uses him as a subchannel to pass the power of the ECK into the world and revitalize it, to make important spiritual changes which will reflect in the social, political, and economic stature of man.

Therefore, the chelas of ECK must not be restless or desirous of changes, but must serve the Living ECK Master wherever he is and wherever it is possible, here and now! The chela must act as a channel for the ECK where it can best be done—at his job, in his home, and in his social environment. He is always working in silence, always open to let the ECK change all his life around him. By being watchful and aware of this, he can see what changes are made.

When the chela eventually becomes a Mahdis, an initiate of the Fifth Circle, he may be chosen to initiate chelas in the name of the ECK Master. The Mahdis must train each ECK chela who is in his ECK Satsang or within his designated area. He must go out among the uninitiated and see that they are in some manner or other led to the Living ECK Master.

It is the duty of the Mahdis to bring those Souls who are ready into ECK to be lifted into the upper regions of pure spirit before the holocaust strikes the worlds of the Kal. The end of this era, the Kali Yuga—the Iron Age, when all is in darkness and ignorance—will come in a few thousand years.

The Mahanta appears again in this world to gather up Souls to return to the true heavenly home. Wherever he goes and whatever he does, the great ECK power clears the way like the whirling winds of a storm. It breaks up the old orders and reestablishes the new within this world. Everywhere the ECK destroys systems established by the Kal forces and injects the spirituality of Soul into the social order and spiritual life of man.

So it is proclaimed that the path of ECK must be taken. A man's lust for possessions and his mad, desperate scramble for material things have become such that the spiritual work of ECK granted by the SUGMAD is the only way; otherwise, this world would be on its way to becoming a veritable desert. Thus the attack on the Kal power continues in the quiet quest for salvation.

It appears that man has been cursed by the SUGMAD because of the standards of living in this world. While man uses up the resources of nature at an alarming rate it is only the natural result of the speeding up of race karma in the last yuga before the destruction of this universe.

It is the last of the yugas, when mankind and his fellow creatures will be destroyed in their respective embodiments, and each Soul lifted into heaven to sleep until the reforming of the lower worlds. Those Souls who have taken up the path of ECK under the Mahanta shall be liberated from this destruction and sleep, and become Co-workers with him.

In the lower worlds, men rule by politics and thereby with orthodox religions. Hence, religions become a system of socio-economics to control man's mind and body. Most world religions have a foundation in the economic systems of their times. Every social order since the start of man in this world has had a religion for its own followers. It has promised the glories of heaven when one dies: suffer on earth and get the reward after death. This is the creed for keeping an exploited society quiet. It has also formed consumer societies throughout history which have created wars and left man in poverty. It has destroyed the natural resources of man and formed a spiritual desert on earth.

As long as this condition exists, man cannot find himself and therefore suffers in spirit. He is ignorant and does not know what has happened to him. He is without a spiritual guide: desperate, seeking and desiring to meet the savior who can halt the wars, bring back the natural resources, and give him comfort in body, mind, and spirit. He has not yet learned that the Living ECK Master awaits his decision to turn to the spiritual path of ECK and find freedom for himself.

All this brings man to the point where he considers himself able to make judgments and form decisions. He is not really able to do this until he has reached the state of the Mahdis. Therefore, he rebels even at calling other men *sir.* This comes from a variation of the title *sire,* which is taken from the word *Sri.* It reflects the early relationship

181

between the spiritual ones who have attained the King-dom of God and those who are still seeking. The efforts of the Mahanta are directed against this sort of relation-ship and against all authority of one man over another. For it is said in ECKANKAR that whosoever puts his hand over another to govern him is an usurper and a tyrant. The ECK declares him an enemy. The Living ECK Master wants no barriers between himself and the chelas of ECKANKAR.

The ECK is always the new-old religion, fitted for the times in which it exists. The human race always needs ECK, for ECK is life itself. This means that ECK is the religion of the people because It is positive in Its effect. There is always the need for ECK because man becomes negative, hence the ECK flows to fit any and all generations.

The proof that the religions of the past are no longer valid can be seen in the performance of the codes of the churches and their priests. Man pays lip service to his churches, synogogues, temples, and mosques, while the life he leads is without ethics.

The ECK chela does not seek utopia, which is the per-fect society, for all things perfect have ceased to grow. The world changes with each generation and man always changes. Hence the concept of utopia, or perfection, is imperfect. This is the mistake made by those who are ruled by Kal Niranjan. They think that once their prom-ised land has been achieved all progress will stop, that their millennium will have been reached. The SUGMAD knows no halting. The path of ECK is forever.

The powers that the SUGMAD may delegate to ITS channel, the Mahanta, are wondrous. Because of the goodness and mercy of the SUGMAD, the Living ECK Master has powers which cannot be comprehended by any average man. He may build, and he may destroy;

but he always maintains an equal balance within the universes where he lives in his many bodies.

Man desires to be entertained instead of seeking out the message of ECK. He is conditioned by the Kal power to seek amusement instead of God. If the wrath of the Mahanta should be incurred, he could speak the word that would bring about the destruction of man's source of amusements, or even man himself. Although it is rare that this would occur, man in his ignorance often attempts to play with the fire of the Mahanta's wrath. This is seeking self-destruction through ignorance.

Man will normally seek God when his struggle for survival on earth is great. When man's economy is lowest, his struggle is greatest, for he believes that his survival is linked with his materialistic life. It is then that his prayers for help are greatest, but they are in vain. He is not asking for the true survival of Soul, but only the survival of his materialistic universe.

But when a civilization has an economy of abundance, man's mind turns away from spiritual survival to publicly provided entertainment. The average man is not capable of programming himself. He cannot think up tasks to occupy himself spiritually, for he has never had to. He has evolved under conditions where the time and energy available to him were programmed for him. There was very seldom time for spiritual things and purely traditional aspects were provided by the church. Festivals were a great relief and source of entertainment. Man never got a chance to become bored with them. He played the games laid down by his church or religion, and this occupied most of his time since the beginning of the history of the human race.

If man is to survive in the physical universe, then he must find time for creative activity in spiritual things. Until this comes about, within a group with time to do something besides subsist in the materialistic worlds, there is little opportunity for the spiritual sensitivity of man to develop. But time spent in contemplation does not automatically produce spiritual results.

In all the civilizations in this world, especially those of the noncreative, average man, mankind has formed for himself predetermined, ritualized activities. This is what can happen to an affluent society, as well as a welfare state, if the leaders do not establish a spiritual or religious time for the common man.

What destroys every social order is the growth of an immense leisure class. It no longer becomes a subsistence culture; other nations must support it. When the populace is offered free food and shelter, the spiritual growth of the nation goes down. Because of this leisure, it gives no incentive for self-programming activities. It usually goes into eclipse as a nation with self-destructive tendencies.

Man always wants something to do, to have some trinket he can play with to take up his leisure time. If he has not the creative abilities to learn Soul Travel, he must come to rely on a government that will see that his leisure time is channeled in the direction to which he is a slave and dependent.

Man does not like to read. It requires that he engage in a great deal of mental activity. He has to visualize the actions from the words, imagine the voice tones and the facial expressions. The average man is not up to such creative labor.

The ECK therefore is what he needs. It is all. Each thing he comes to learn is the ECK. The bird singing in the tree is ECK. It is transcending and descending all in the same motion. As It descends, It also transcends and vice versa. Truth is for those who know, those who come to know and never question it. They realize that questions are never satisfying and never answered.

"He who loves me will love me for what I am. He who hates me shall hate me for what I am not. Those who question all the works of ECK shall never know Truth and shall always be bothered with questions. None shall ever know Truth. It is not possible to have Truth and at the same time ask questions about it," says the SUGMAD.

Thus it is that the ECK Satsang is really the key to the spiritual works of ECKANKAR. So long as the Satsangs have sufficient chelas who are open as channels for the ECK to reach the non-ECKists within their communities, nations, and on all levels of consciousness, then will the ECK survive.

Therefore, the Satsangs become absolutely important to the collective body of the chelas, as each forms an enormous channel which can control the spiritual affairs of this world and the worlds beyond. As a collective body the Satsang brings harmony, peace, and happiness to the individual, and to all entities within the universes of God.

This is the real secret of the works of ECK, and as long as the ECK Satsangs hold their related positions, none can be resolved by the Kal power but only by the Mahanta. Defeat of the power of the ECK Satsangs will never take place, for any attempt to do so does not make the slightest impression on the Satsang and the chela concerned.

The Light and Sound of ECK therefore uses the Mahanta as the major channel for Its work within the worlds of God. It is through the Mahanta that the chela may be established in the ECK Satsang or act alone as the channel through which the Mahanta works in this world.

Man has been taught to want certain things in this materialistic world. Now he must reverse himself, for since he has solved the problem of the production of abundance, he must now take stock and work out his path to his destiny, which is ECKANKAR. The overwhelming majority of mankind is working either on methods of destruction, or on the creation of new products which people do not actually need or want. Instead, mankind should be working on spiritual unfoldment: the curing of man's ills, delving into the secrets of life, plumbing the ocean's depths, and reaching out to the world of God through Soul Travel.

The words of the Mahanta alone can change the world, completely and irrevocably. He is the only being who has developed his spiritual perception beyond any point known in the history of the human race. Generally, he contacts those who are ECK chelas, but there are many times when he communicates with whole groups of people or individuals outside his own followers. So often he uses an ECK chela as a channel to pass on a thought to a large body of persons within a certain area. He is always in contact with every ECK Satsang or collective body of Souls, as well as with every ECK chela on a personal and individual basis.

If he so desires, the Living ECK Master can make spiritual contact with the whole of mankind or all beings in any country at any time, regardless of language barriers. He can make contact with any entity on any plane, regardless of which plane. He keeps the inhabitants on every plane throughout the universe intact and working on mutually common causes, whether or not the causes have the appearance of ECK to the outer senses. Yet the ECK is the underlying factor, the essence of life, which only the Mahdis can recognize in all languages, religions, and philosophies everywhere. All life therefore flows out of the ECK; and all religions, philosophies, and sacred writings are based upon the ECK and Its original source, called the Shariyat-Ki-Sugmad.

Races and persons at different levels of consciousness will divide the ECK into various parts because of their lower states of thought and spiritual development. Few have the level of consciousness to accept the ECK. This is the reason why many fail to understand and grasp Its meaning.

Few can understand and know what the ECK may do. It is so vast, so magnificent in Its scope. The select few who come to It are actually the most fortunate of all the followers of the spiritual paths. These Souls are fortunate because they have come to the apex of their training in the lower worlds and have passed the tests established by the SUGMAD and administered by Kal Niranjan. They are indeed fortunate, for now, after long centuries of spiritual training and incarnations, they have reached their last life on earth and have come under the guidance of the Mahanta.

He takes them under his wing in loving care and is thereafter with them wherever they may be, whether it is on this plane or any of those in the heavenly worlds. He always stays with those whom he has given the initiation into ECK, whether that person has left this physical body or not. It is also generally known that the Mahanta may stay with his own chelas, those he has initiated on earth or the spiritual worlds, whether he himself has passed on from this life or not.

Man will go nearly insane if he cannot label everything. He simply must have an explanation for all things. Three-quarters of the human race spends its time wandering about aimlessly. The Living ECK Master comes forth from out of the secrecy of his existence, whenever man needs to be pulled out of the dark ages.

Human character is determined by environment rather than heredity. Human faults are imparted by bad training and karma. The vices of the young spring not from the Kal; they are derived from the defects of spiritual training in this life and past lives.

Mystery is not a satisfactory term to describe the experience of God. It is only an intimation of something more profoundly significant, often recognized in a flash. But an understanding of its significance does not always follow such an experience in one's life. The curtain, unnoticed, is sometimes moved aside, and other curtains also, so that Soul can see Its own self and thus reveal the mystery of what It truly is. Then the curtain drops in place again and a measure of oblivion descends.

God has had thousands of names, but none of them is apt. This Reality has sometimes been called the good, beautiful, and true, to name a few. Philosophers term IT the Absolute, or Ultimate, Reality. Western mystics say IT is the Godhead, and in general know it as God. IT is Brahma and Paramatma to the Hindus; the Beloved of the Sufis; the Tao, or Way, of the Chinese mystics. The Buddhists say IT is Nirvana. But none of these is the true reality of the SUGMAD. This is the ultimate of all realities. IT is the Ultimate, and is so far above all things that few ever achieve IT.

There is no name for this True Reality, for names set boundaries. Therefore, all the above that are known by name are within the world of the Kal. Those which are listed here, with the exception of the SUGMAD, are only Fourth Plane phenomena. If something can be labeled, it is still within the world of the mind, the Fourth Plane, which is the final region still under the influence of Kal Niranjan.

This is why the SUGMAD takes as ITS name the Ocean of Love and Mercy: the world of the unknown, the unknown ITSELF.

Mystics and poets are generally introverts and do not have good relationships with the outer worlds. They are supremely fortunate in that visions of reality sometimes come to them unsought. But they are even more fortunate if they are able to induce these visions.

The extroverts are not so fortunate, for generally, when they glimpse this reality of God, they are so shocked into fearing for their sanity that they will back away without any further contact. They are also uncomfortable in the presence of anyone who has had such experiences and can handle them. They will label such an experience a mental abberation or go to see their physician.

When one is concerned with the pure element of the divine reality, he finds no words to speak of IT, for IT cannot be set apart from ITSELF. To say IT is material in nature is to label IT, to play with words.

Man's consciousness cannot be easily divested of symbols. The mystics use all sorts of terms such as divine bliss, infinite love, and others. But the labels are merely those of the mind trying to grasp what is unknown to it. This has been done for centuries and is not limited to any faith, religion, person, creed, or cult. The ECK has been found in many parts of the world, from the beginning of time to the present, having made Itself known to some but not to others.

The ECK never plays favorites but always reveals some portion of Itself to those who are persistent and obey the instructions laid down by the Living ECK Master. So many times Its concern is with the economics and politics of nations in which Its mystics are inhabitants, but this usually turns out to be a phenomenon of the Mental Plane.

The ECKist who reaches the stages beyond the level of phenomenon becomes intoxicated with visions of the True Reality, and he no longer cares for conventional forms. He grows beyond propriety, religion, philosophy, economics, and other materialistic forms which become suffocating to him.

If the cynic believes the esoteric experiences of divine

189

reality are illusions, he must suffer for his ignorance. No ECKist who has had intense or prolonged experiences doubts the validity of them. But what is brought forth from the initiated is difficult to communicate to those who are the uninitiated. Life, as it is in the materialistic worlds, sadly rejects the experiences of the ECKist, and the validity of the Living ECK Master.

Therefore, we find that all ECKists, regardless of their spiritual status and nationality, are still disciples of ECKANKAR. Whether the chela is living on the Physical Plane or the Atma Lok (the Soul Plane), he never feels he is in a separate world, or state. He is still under the general authority of the ECK, and the individual laws of the separate planes are to be obeyed, and homage paid to their various rulers and spiritual governors. He does not feel like either a citizen or an alien, but rather like a modern traveler who goes through each country as a tourist or for business.

The entities of each plane look upon their existence there as sort of a contract of service. This is the way it should be, for whether they consciously realize it or not, all are actually the children of the ECK kingdom. In this way it makes no difference what religion or path Soul may adopt for Itself, It is a full citizen of the kingdom of ECK. All Souls belong to this kingdom, whether they desire it to be so or not. The longer they resist this, the longer anyone withstands the ECK, the longer they continue their existence on the Awagawan, the Wheel of the Eighty-Four. Since the beginning of time, all Souls—regardless of their faith, creed, religion, philosophy, cult, or sect—have had the consolation that they are full citizens of the kingdom of ECK.

Servitude on earth in the human form, or in any of the psychic planes, is a small price to pay if it purchases a ticket to the true Kingdom of God, which is by the way of ECKANKAR.

The ECKist finds there is only one Mahanta at a time within all the universes. All other ECK Masters in the Order of the Vairagi, the Brotherhood of ECK Masters, are known as the Maharaj.

Every Maharaj is subordinate to the Mahanta, the Living ECK Master, no matter who he might be, for the Mahanta holds the ECK Rod of Power. It is given to him on the twenty-second day of October. The Mahanta holds this Rod of Power until he translates or passes the Rod of ECK Power to his successor and takes an esoteric position within the Order of the Vairagi somewhere in the universes as a spiritual worker of great importance. Then he too becomes subordinate to the next Mahanta, or Living ECK Master. He becomes a member of the spiritual hierarchy, where before he was the head of it and responsible directly to the SUGMAD.

Besides the Maharajs, there are the Mahavakyis, who are known as the Silent Ones, for they have charge of all the universes and the affairs on each plane. All Souls within all universes are within their orbit of affairs. Their duties are to see that every Soul, regardless of Its spiritual status, has the opportunity to enter into the Kingdom of God here and now. It makes little difference which plane the Soul is on. It depends on the individual Soul to do what It will with the opportunity presented to It. All the Soul has to do is recognize the opportunity, thereby forgetting any religion, creed, or faith he has followed, knowing that each was only a step on the way to ECK, the true pathway to God. One then learns that every Soul living somewhere in the universes of God is actually a follower of ECK.

Unless the individual has planted his feet directly on the path under the guidance of the Mahanta, then he has wasted time and effort. The lower paths of philosophies and religions are necessary but none will last forever.

Soon he will find that upon reaching certain spiritual levels, he will be able to meet with the Living ECK Master and resolve all his problems both spiritually and physically. He will find that all religions, faiths, and philosophies are merely necessary steps to reach the ECK. It is all part of the overall omnipresence of the ECK. Nothing can exist but for the ECK, and unless one has himself rightly placed within the ECK, knowing It for what It is, then he is still on the treadmill of the Kal.

He will find that philosophy is merely a psychic means of studying religions through the intellect. He will know that religion is the means which the Kal has established to take control of the masses. Kal puts emphasis upon the mind and body consciousness so that Soul cannot express Itself freely. It is only when one goes beyond the intellect into the spiritual arenas that the ECK is truly known.

The ECK is the true reality, that shining essence of the SUGMAD which cannot be found by worldly eyes, senses, and perceptions. It is only found in the true self, that which is known as Soul. With the ECK comes the Sound of the flute of the SUGMAD. This is what Soul is, and none can deprive Soul of It once It has been experienced. It is something beyond words and sounds, symbols and signs.

Until Soul returns again to this state of consciousness, It will always struggle in the meshes of the Kal. It is the purpose of the Kal power to keep Soul trapped until It learns Truth and starts on the path to perfection, the path of ECKANKAR. These are the responsibilities and the mission which God assigned Kal Niranjan.

11

The Way of ECK Perfection

The very reason why most occult, metaphysical, and spiritual writings (including the sacred works of the orthodox religions) in this world fail is that too many who write them never realize that knowledge alone is not wisdom. A catalog of facts and opinions by itself does not constitute either literature or perfected works of any nature.

Most Oriental religious literature and most Western sacred works lie mainly in the field of knowledge and historical facts. Some parts, of course, contain wisdom, but generally they are only legends and myths expressed in poetic form; they are merely stating what the writer wants the orthodox followers and readers to believe.

The sacred mystery of the ECK lies in the initiation of the Ninth Circle, for when one comes to this level of spiritual growth he does not wish to live in this life anymore. He becomes dead, only to awaken when the body dies. He sees nothing in the sacred writings of orthodox religions and does not wish to read them or refer to them again. He seeks no glory, no titles in this life, and will reject all those given him. He becomes honest to the point of pain for himself and cannot find happiness in anything in this world. He has no interest in social reform nor any wish to bring about adjustments in this life for the masses; he only wants to see that each Soul has the opportunity to gain salvation through ECK.

ECK does not pose as a remedy for the illnesses of this world, but is only a path to spiritual freedom. The Mahanta can change the world and its history but there is little likelihood that he would ever do this. Every Living ECK Master has come to this world to impart spirituality to a materialistic age. He gives an extra spiritual push to every era of mankind. But there is always a fixed time for such divine workings, and when the time is ripe, the Living ECK Master who has made his appearance in this world during each respective age of mankind reveals his true nature to the world. Not one has differed in this essential doctrine.

The chief commandments of ECK, running like a golden thread through the teachings of every Living ECK Master, have all been based upon the teachings of the SUGMAD. These divine ones come out into the public when their help is most needed, when spirituality is at its lowest ebb in some country of the world or planet, and materialism is apparently victorious.

Each Living ECK Master in his respective time, has laid down the spiritual law again and again to help those who follow the path of ECK. These laws, which are truth, have always existed to lead man to God. But the priestcraft has taken the laws of ECK and made them into tenets for organized religions. Therefore the idealistic spirit and the motivating force that prevailed during the time of each Living ECK Master all but disappeared under the weight of orthodox dogma.

Therefore, the Living ECK Masters have always had the responsibility to not establish new religions, cults, or mystery schools. Instead they rejuvenate the religious thoughts of all people, instilling a higher understanding of life into them.

The founders of dogmatic religions usually passed away, leaving little. Later somebody would invent dogma from the words the founder preached, and a religion is established. All religions, regardless of what they are and who founded them, are from the same source, the ECK.

ECK is life itself, the Audible Life Stream. The time is coming that will bring ECK to the world as a universal spiritual belief. Mankind will accept It. ECK will serve all races of people and all countries. The way is being prepared to enable the Mahanta to deliver the worldwide message.

This will come when there is total chaos and confusion everywhere, when the world is rocking in upheavals, earthquakes, floods, and volcanic eruptions; when both east and west are aflame with war. Then is he needed most by all mankind. The whole world must suffer, for the whole world must be redeemed.

When such conditions are at their worst, the Living ECK Master will make himself publicly known and will declare his mission to the entire world. He shall, by his spiritual powers, speedily bring all conflicts to an abrupt end, bringing peace once more to all nations. Then mankind will rest from all conflicts, on all planets within the world system.

No one should require the Living ECK Master to fit into that person's image of what a spiritual giant might be. Few ECK Masters will ever fit the popular image of what the masses think is a Godman. ECK Masters act too independently of the general social concept, doing as they wish, and usually living a life of their own and never bothering anyone.

The problem existing among the orthodox religions is

a lack of understanding on their part that destroys communications. It is not that disciples of any orthodox religion lack an opportunity to communicate, but most are intolerant of ECK. Most orthodox followers believe only in their traditional faith. This gives each, they think, all the answers to life and its problems. Therefore they refuse to accept any ECK chela's point of view. This is a trap of the Kal force and is dangerous in the lower worlds.

Thus the ECK chela must proceed with caution when he wishes to pass the message of ECK to others. Few want to listen because they have been steeped in their religious traditions and believe that everything else is wrong. Their founder's name has become a part of the woof and warp of their lives, and if anyone speaks of anything being greater than him, there is danger. This is why it is courageous to be an ECKist. But the ECKist must sacrifice and go forth to spread the message of ECKANKAR.

He knows there are dangers because the Kal force will use any of those who are wrapped in orthodox religions to get rid of him. They will do it in some manner or other, if at all possible. But the ECKist must know that life alone cannot teach him all that he wants to know about ECK. He knows though that if the ECK uses him as a channel all will be well. Consequently, he cares little for what happens to his human body, for nothing can stop him. He cares little if all things in his material world are taken away. If he loses everything but himself, nothing matters but spreading the message of ECK.

The strange influence of the Mahanta on all who see him in person, or as a spiritual being when they can open their spiritual eye and see him in the Atma body, is indeed fascinating. Those who can feel reverence for the spiritual quality in him without belief in ECK are indeed rare. But ignorance of his spiritual greatness does

196

not bar materialistic persons from tasting the radiant influence of spirituality emanating from him.

Those who come to the Living ECK Master and say that they are inclined to follow his teachings are told to associate with those who have had spiritual experiences. Contact with such persons will assist in bringing out the latent spirituality in anyone. Those who have had such experiences are usually the Mahdis, the initiates of the Fifth Plane. Therefore, the society of such people is very important as the first step, and often it is the last, as the Mahanta often will say to seekers of the SUGMAD.

The Mahdis are above the Mental Plane, therefore they are not to practice magic. This includes both black and white magic, for the practitioner will come to regret it if he does. He will learn that the use of magic for anything, regardless of what it might be, will bring effects that are not good. If he uses it to heal others or to injure anyone, then it is wrong. In healing anyone with a bodily affliction it is the ECK that does so, not the magic which is part of the Universal Mind Power, or that known as the Kal force.

When the Mahdis reaches this level of spiritual unfoldment, he must then begin to let the ECK use him completely as a channel. Then he starts to become all things to all people. To those under the law he becomes as one under the law, though not being himself under the law. To those outside the law he becomes as one outside the law. To the weak he becomes weak, and to the strong he becomes strong. Therefore, he becomes all things to all men in order to help and possibly lead some to the Mahanta, the Living ECK Master.

Life for the Mahdis becomes a cinema play, unrolling its episodes from the cradle to the grave. Instead of seeking truth through any of the psychic means, he looks for the real, the enduring, the eternal principles of ECK. He does not look for ECK in the illusionary for It is never there.

The power of ECK can conquer any aberration of life. Millions labor under the illusion that their emptiness, their guilt, and their lack of purpose are due to their material and environmental associations. If any lack a spiritual purpose in ECK, then life will become dull for them. It is contemplation and belief in the Mahanta that can bring about a new life.

It is only the Mahanta who can cleanse Soul and forgive all that has been created in this world of materialistic values. The Mahanta gives each Soul a new challenge and purpose. He brings about the imperishable things which man has created for himself. When the chela has taken away all his false concepts of life and sees only the divine sense, then he no longer runs after another man's opinion. He understands and knows truth.

Whosoever looks deeply into himself and perceives only discontent, frailty, darkness, and fear need not be afraid nor curl his lips in scorn. But let him seek the Mahanta, who can be found within his heart. It is then that he will become aware of the ECK and Its purposes for him. He will learn that his own divine nature will reveal Itself in him, and that he will no longer walk indifferently. He will learn that no one is excluded from the divine nature of the ECK consciousness, that it is only man that excludes himself from It.

It is the man who thinks he may live as freely as his unconsidered desires prompt him who does not see the reckoning of such an attitude. He is binding his life to a hollow dream if he persists in this thought. If he has had the experience of knowing his true self, there will never be any hatred for another.

Anyone with ego-consciousness often confuses this with self-knowledge or Self-Realization. He takes it for granted that if he has ego-consciousness then he knows himself. But the ego knows only its own contents, not the true self and Its contents. It knows only human and psychic knowledge, and only too often those in this ego-conscious state measure their knowledge by what the average person in their social environment understands. Psychic and social facts are for the most part what makes up the human psyche. One is always coming up against the prejudice that such a thing as Self-Realization could not happen with him or in his environment. And on the other hand, he meets with equally illusory assumptions that merely serve to cover up the true facts of such cases.

The concept of unity which is supposed to embrace the universe and all its action, is titanic in scope and potential. He who dares to examine this concept soon discovers that it leads into something too great for understanding, for it leads to the ECK. An alternative becomes imperative, for if he is an extremist he abandons normal life to become a hermit. If he finds this too impossible, he rejects his ideal completely and lives the unexamined life with all its unhappy consequences. The only good solution, both personally and socially, then, is compromise. Man must particularize and reduce his god to a form that he can handle, thereby distorting and sometimes obliterating the original image.

When man is allowed to proceed naturally with the reduction of the image of his god, the image will conform to the social and political expectations of the civilization of his times. Every major religion in the world has evolved a hundred species to fit man's image of the various types of gods that he seeks. All this attests to the needs of man for what is known as the examined life. These compromises are vitiated by the panaceas that lead to dogma. But if anyone should recognize the fallacies in the dogma of the orthodox religions, he usually comes into an understanding of the ECK.

Man insists upon talk and exposition but the ECK cannot be put into words. Sometimes, however, a profusion of images and metaphors are used by the ECK Masters. The problem here, however, is that a spoken language is the expression of the Kal, and it presents a hardship of how to get a positive image in the demonstration of ECK to this world.

Philosophy and worldly religion describe the SUGMAD in negative language. Neither deny IT but both are too often emphatic that the existence of Reality is not true. Actually, there is no vocabulary that can express the truth of the existence of Reality. Reality is Truth, though the ECK chela finds so many interpretations of truth that he cannot help being confused. He tries to get into the heart of truth, but it always eludes him in some manner because he cannot get a mental grasp of it. This is the problem of language: it exists only on the mental realm to express itself vocally to the external world. Since Truth is beyond the mental realm, it cannot be grasped except through the internal vision.

This is why ECKANKAR can be described as the Everlasting Gospel. It is not available to the senses of the Buddhi, the function of the mind that discriminates and decides. Chitta, the function which takes note of form and beauty, sees these things in truth but is unable to pass them along to the Buddhi. Manas, the other function of the mind called the mind stuff, the Universal Mind Power, only has the power to receive feeling and taste. But the Buddhi, being thought, must discriminate and decide what is best to give to the outer world as a good representation of itself.

Thus, if not governed by Soul, the mind does not allow for anything but itself. It causes man in the masses to find dynamic living too difficult and fatiguing. The average man requests codification of life; he looks for laws to live by and for somebody to provide them. To reach out for anything beyond this is too much for his senses and his understanding. This is what makes the ECKist a special person, for he is in the ECK and lives in dynamic dimensions. He knows that peace does not come when an oligarchy, a government, or some ruler decrees peace, nor does order come through ossified rituals of legislation.

Every ECKist knows that this sort of external peace and order will sooner or later flounder, creating difficulties and eventual destruction for itself. It has nothing to do with the SUGMAD and ITS works. It is something which the Kal uses to exploit the masses for its own interest, for behind all this is the Kal, trying to trap the mind of every individual Soul.

Belief in a creed is not always due to religious feeling, but is more often a social matter. As such, it does nothing to give the individual values to live by. For support he must depend exclusively on his relation with the ECK, an authority which is not of this world. No lofty principles nor creeds of orthodox religions can lay a spiritual foundation for the ECK chela. It is simply empirical awareness, the incontrovertible experience of an intensely personal, reciprocal relationship between the chela and the Mahanta. This has nothing to do with either the physical world, reason, or logic, as human consciousness knows them. But it does have everything to do with the ECK consciousness.

A clear distinction must be made between what is essential in ECKANKAR and what is haphazard. The ECK doctrine has naturally been preserved in a form suited to those Souls It could reach since the beginning of the universes. This is especially true in the lower worlds.

Many have been called but few are able to comprehend

and understand the ECK. Those Souls who do are then consciousnesses that are open to the ECK for gaining awareness. They serve in the lower worlds, or wherever Soul is needed.

Every ECK chela must grasp the tools of the spiritual works of ECKANKAR in the field of mystical experiences. He must know there are two types of spiritual experience, both of which are found in the works of ECK. First is the extrovertive spiritual experience, and second is the introvertive type. Both are attempts at the apprehension of the full experience of the divine Reality. But they are reached in different ways.

The extrovertive way looks outward, through the physical senses into the external world, finding there the greater experience of the divine Reality. The introvertive way turns inward, with an introspective manner of seeing through the inner senses and eyes to find the greater experience of the divine Reality beyond the human consciousness. Naturally, this type of experience should outweigh the extrovertive way in importance. In the course of human history the introvertive way becomes a major resource to depend upon for decisions and changes of events and nations.

The extroverted seeker with his physical manner, including the five external senses, will perceive the same world of trees, hills, concrete roads, and household furniture as most people generally do. But he sees something which the average person does not see. He observes that these objects are transformed into something through which the ECK shines to illuminate his senses. So many of those who have been called mystics and seekers of God have found the spiritual experience of life in blades of grass, wood, and stone. These types of extrovertive mystics have always pointed out that God is in everything.

The extrovertive seeker has the ability to know and

separate the ECK from the material things of life, yet he can see that the ECK is the very substance of all life in such things. This puts him above the average man who has a lesser understanding, which does not qualify him to see the ECK as the whole or everyday life as the divine Reality.

This understanding of the extrovertive mystic passes beyond the sensory-intellectual consciousness into the conceptual intellect. However, the distinction between the ECK and these things has not wholly disappeared. The extrovertive mystic is generally one who finds all things identical—such as grass being the same as stone—although each is different. Mostly these extroverts are the poets, metaphysicians, and religious writers.

What they are saying is a complete paradox, in fact contradictory. But paradox is one of the common characteristics of mysticism. Paradoxes arise because the chela is dealing with the elements of psychic power, better known as the Kal force. The Kal always deals in mystery and paradox, for everything in its universe consists of dichotomies. The Kal is always presenting the two sides of the coin in order to bring about confusion and complexity. This is what causes any mystic to question the affairs of the SUGMAD. Dichotomies always bring questions, because few within the human consciousness understand the two-sided view of life.

The mystic is not an ECKist, and neither is an ECKist ever a mystic. The mystic is one who has never gone beyond the Mental worlds. He deals in the mystification of the spirito-psychic worlds. The true worlds of the SUGMAD, which lie above the Atma Lok, have no complication nor mystery. They are what they are; the whole element of these worlds is simply Truth. When one has moved into these worlds and placed himself upon one of these planes, he is therefore part of them and never questions. All things are as they are because it is proper and fitting for them to be this way.

He never questions, never indulges in the mystification of life, but leaves all things as they are. He knows that the extrovertive mystic is simply a psychic who has gained a little more insight than most seekers, and that he is halfway on the path to reaching the Fifth Plane. This is the experience of the sensory-intellectual. He sees only what has been granted him: a perception of the world as being transfigured and unified in a single reality. Some identify this single reality as God and others do not, but it all ties in with the same thing, the ECK. In most societies, however, this type of experience leads to pantheism. Nevertheless, the experience of the extrovert is important in making headway on the path of ECK. Yet it is not the end of the road, as so many believe.

The success of the introvertive experience depends on shutting out all physical sensations from one's consciousness. Average men believe this to be easy. One can shut one's eyes, cover one's ears, and hold the nose. He can avoid taste sensations by keeping the mouth closed and empty. But no one can simply shut off the tactile sensations, for it is difficult to be rid of organic sensations. But this is what the chela must learn to do to enjoy the subjective, that is, the introvertive experience. He must learn to thrust tactile and organic sensations out of his conscious awareness, into the unconscious. Neither does he go to the trouble of holding his nose, stopping his eyes, and emptying his mouth. The only thing he does is close his eyes and close out all organic sensations.

After this is done, the chela then drops all sensuous images from his mind. This is the most difficult part of the contemplative exercises, but it is possible. After this, one stops the thinking and reasoning processes within himself. Having gotten rid of the whole empirical content of sensations, images, thoughts, and presumably all emotions, he will find that his desires and volitions will disappear, since they normally exist only as attachments to cognitive awareness.

All consciousness of his human self will then have disappeared. Often the chela will go to sleep when this happens, or become unconscious. The total suppression of the whole content of human consciousness is what the introvertive mystic claims to be able to achieve. He claims that the sensory-intellectual consciousness disappears and is replaced by an entirely new kind of consciousness, which he calls the mystical consciousness. Although the yogis and many of the Eastern mystics use this modus operandi, it turns out to be the wrong way to reach the spiritual consciousness. There is a difference between spiritual consciousness and mystical consciousness. The former is the highest, when one reaches and enters into the state above the Atma Lok, the Fifth Plane. The latter is only reached when one enters into the Mental realm.

Samadhi, a mystical state of consciousness, belongs in this area of the psychic worlds. But Nirvikalpa, a spiritual state of consciousness, belongs in the area of the true ECK worlds. This leads to detachment, which eventually takes the chela through the varied initiations into the Ninth, when he becomes a member of the Order of Vairagi, the ECK Masters.

When one reaches the Samadhi state of consciousness he becomes one with the Kal, but it appears to him that he is one with the Divine Source of Life, the SUGMAD. This is why many have said that the Godhead is pure nothingness, a desert and a wilderness. Here again the mystic is talking in metaphors that are useless to the chela.

The chela needs no such explanation of the SUGMAD and the ECK, for within the worlds of the true spiritual universe, It is Light and Sound. This is all there is. One does not need to find explanations for the Light and Sound, for there are none. Soul knows and understands instantly what goes on in the worlds of the SUGMAD, and never questions. Soul just knows and does not call this knowing either religion or philosophy.

In the study of inner world experiences, most men believe that the mystical experience and the religious experience are the same; and actually, neither of these are the same as the ECK experience. There is an important connection between mysticism and religion, but it is not nearly so direct and immediate as most people seem to think.

The mystical experience has been described here. The experience of the religionist is of some undifferentiated unity which is often interpreted as union with God. But this is only the interpretation and is not the experience itself. The great problem here is that most Souls do not have a sufficiently analytical faculty to distinguish between the experience and the interpretation. The ECKist usually has the proper training, so that when he comes into an experience of this nature, he is able to distinguish between the real, the pseudoreal, and the unreal.

The introvertive experience often gives the experiencer the feeling of melting away into infinity. The religionist will experience a blazing light which seems to be the center of all things. But each is only reaching the same point in the high Mental Plane, and is being deceived by the Kal Niranjan into believing this is God. The ECKist enters into the Atma Lok, the Fifth Plane, with the assistance of the Living ECK Master. He is not at all misled by the Kal into believing that the Brahm world, the Mental Plane is the ultimate of all planes. Neither does he believe that the Saguna Brahm Plane, which is the unconscious world, is the last of the path. He knows

206

that the path of ECK ends in the SUGMAD. He will strive onward until reaching this world, this Ocean of Love and Mercy. Nothing will or can hold him back, for it is the guidance of the Living ECK Master which takes him into the highest worlds of all, where he receives his spiritual mission and becomes a Co-worker with the SUGMAD.

Whether the seeker understands it or not, it is true that the mystical experience will bring him into intimate association with the religion, culture, and the civilization of his times. It does not have any tendency to make him a member of any particular creed or sect; it will not basically change his traits. If he is a Hindu, he will remain a Hindu. If a Buddhist, he will remain a Buddhist.

He will believe in whatever is the scripture of his particular society and civilization. His background and religious tendencies will be part of the culture to which he belongs, and his faith in the religious scriptures of his country will be the guidepost and the strength for his spiritual drive. The framework of which creed he will fit his experience into will depend mostly on the culture in which he lives.

However, it will be found on close scrutiny that most seekers are using mysticism merely as an escape from life and from its duties and responsibilities. The mystic can retreat into a private ecstacy of bliss, turning his back on the world and forgetting not only his sorrow, but the needs and sorrows of his fellowmen. His life becomes narrow and selfish.

The preoccupation of man in his waking state is for comforts and for survival as long as possible; he looks for any state that gives him joy, regardless of whether it is a mystical state or a state of material comfort. He lives through periods of skepticism and drops his skepticism when he feels that the comfort states are leaving him.

When such states of comfort are regained, he once more

establishes himself in the persistent ideal of ease and happiness with his materiality. He knows, lives, and is aware of life as the part of his physical and human senses. Other than this there is little else in life for him. He accumulates material possessions and gives back to life the least he can, but always in hopes that it will return him greater rewards.

The evolution of his consciousness is always slow. It takes many lives to reach anyone of this nature. He goes through the evolution of life in matter, and the evolution of life in mind power. But to him the ECK is only a word which merely states the spiritual phenomena of life without explaining them. Neither is it any good for him because he has to extend himself and gains little, according to the material world. Life then becomes a form of veiled consciousness. He objects to stepping any further into a more evolved state.

Thus, the ECK is not a doctrine, It is a perspective. It is not a philosophy, but a mood. It is not the ECKist who makes ECK, but the ECK which makes the ECKist; and this ECK is all of life.

The materialist is one who always sees the variety and not the reality of life, who wanders on from birth to rebirth trying to find what might be the answers to his permanent desire for creature comforts. The ECKist finds that whosoever wants life shall live, and whosoever wants love shall have love. But whosoever wants hatred shall suffer through the hardships and pangs of discomfort from death to death, through life after life.

The ECKist need not ask what to do with his life and his efforts in life, for the ECK engulfs him constantly and gives him task after task. He becomes a conduit through which flows an electric current of power. This current becomes him, until he can no longer feel the difference between It and himself. He cannot recognize where It begins in him and leaves off in him; It compels him to accept Itself for whatever It might be. It is the ECK power, using him as a channel.

After he has accepted It as part of himself and allows It to use him, his life cannot be otherwise. He wants It to continue to use him as a channel, and keeps himself open to the ECK at all times.

The lower self must learn that it cannot exist in eternity, as it belongs to Kal Niranjan. Since Soul does not belong in the lower worlds except to live in them temporarily, then all Its communication should be with the ECK.

No problem is given man which is greater than himself. Each being is tested according to his capacity; none are tested beyond it. Each problem which man encounters has a spiritual solution, and each person has his troubles at the point where he is most negative and vulnerable.

Whosoever knows one thing therefore knows fully all things, for Truth in one spiritual thing is inseparable from the Truth of all things. If one knows himself then he has Self-Realization; but if he knows a single factor about Truth, he certainly knows all Truth. The mind of man and the mind in man are One. This is the law of the lower worlds, and that which so often betrays the seeker of the divine.

Man should never seek to become one with God, for he is then falling victim to Kal Niranjan. He is catering to the impermanent and not to that which is eternal. Only the SUGMAD is eternal, and can give life in the eternity. What men call God is impermanent and cannot give life to any except in the psychic worlds.

By trying to bring together the lower self and the higher self to make them one, in order to enter into the worlds of ECK, is to bring about defeat. They do not mix, for none are as far apart in poles as these two qualities. The lower represents the Kal which is the negative power, and Soul represents the ECK which is the higher power. The twain shall never meet, for the lower, being of the Universal Mind Power, must step aside and be left behind so that Soul can enter into the heavenly worlds.

Spirituality and the sciences of man are also separated by the same factor. Spirituality represents the highest in man and the universe, while science is only representative of the negative or materialistic. Mind does not seek truth but only the material and what is needed to survive in the world of Kal Niranjan.

All that is life is the ECK. Thus the eternal paradox and eternal truth of ECK is within all. It is only the chela who has the insight to look into life and find the ECK behind all things, working slowly and quietly to bring about the spiritual change which is the true purpose of the SUGMAD.

12

The Sacred Works of ECKANKAR

Every chela of ECK is a special person. He is special because all his protection is from the Living ECK Master. Though he has been under the protection of the Mahanta for many centuries, yet has ignored his presence, it does not keep him from receiving the Mahanta's blessings.

The ECK chela is always cherished, beloved, and protected by the ECK Master in every act of the chela's life. He is taken care of in every possible way, furnished with life, love, and the generosity and kindness of the Living ECK Master. The chela does not have to call upon the Living ECK Master to fulfill any needs in his life, for everything is taken care of without request.

Desires are the least of the chela's worry, for he is never without the protection of the Living ECK Master. There are times when he may feel that he is in disfavor, but this is never true. The Living ECK Master may stand aside and let the chela go through a certain test because he needs the experience. The Mahanta is always testing the chela in one way or other, for he knows that this is the way to keep the chela aware and always watchful of what life may bring him. Sometimes it is pain, for pain is often the creator of awareness, and sometimes it is hardship, but if the chela will recognize this, he will know that he is most fortunate, for the Mahanta is merely putting him through some karma in order to reach a higher level.

Most fortunate is the chela who receives the blessings of the Mahanta in some manner or other. If the Mahanta touches the chela with the tip of his finger, shakes hands with him, or kisses him, the gift of the Lord is passed from ECK Master to chela. The Master is only the medium, or channel, by which the blessing is passed from the SUGMAD to the chela.

The chela must be spiritually developed to such a high degree that he inspires a subtle peace of mind and serenity of heart in those who are the noninitiated. He must give joy to those around himself. Dignity and sweet humility are the twin traits of the ECK chela, and he cannot be otherwise. He is ready to go forth to preach the gospel of ECK to the world, revealing Its secrets to those who are ready to listen. He will show that the Mahanta is the divine one who has taken upon himself the human frame for the emancipation of Souls.

The Living ECK Master alone connects one with the ECK, the Sound Current. He is the incarnation eternally present on earth for this purpose, and he knows who is ready here and now. The chela, in his work to assist the spiritual ECK Master, finds that men are hopelessly immersed and imprisoned in mind and maya. Seeing the true Mahanta within the form of the outer body brings salvation and permanently puts an end to all unworthy desires.

As moths are drawn to the flames and hummingbirds to the honeysuckle, so the nonbeliever is drawn to the chela, who in turn is drawn to the Mahanta. Without being drawn to the Mahanta in this way the inner fires of faith are never kindled and devotion never aroused. Without these, no grace may ever be bestowed by the Mahanta, and the goal of Ultimate Reality never gained.

The body is the temple in which Soul dwells while on earth. It is transient and perishable; subject to birth, growth, decay, and death. The senses of the body often lead the individual astray so that he follows the false teachers, prophets, and pseudomasters. These are only the Kal working through the lower forces.

The ECK must be first in the thought and deeds of every ECK chela. Until he has reached this stage of life, all things seem useless to him. However, all else must be forgotten. Only ECK should be first in his life. Life becomes worthless, damaging, and without any meaning whatsoever, if he has not accepted ECK as the supreme reality in himself.

The chela's stream of consciousness, which is a worldly concept of thought as a continuous procession of experiences and memories through time, must be imbued with the ECK. It must be filled with everything that is the ECK, instead of those forces which are known as the Kal power, or the lower world psychic things. One has to bring himself into agreement with the ECK and not the Kal forces. When he has reached a certain agreement with the ECK, this stream of consciousness pouring through his mind will be changed to make him a channel of the divine reality.

The jumble of thoughts pouring through the individual's mind are from habit. They have tremendous influence on the individual, and certainly are not truth at all, but only the reflection of the nature of Kal. Often, by picking out a thought here and there to verbalize, one sees that thoughts are often a stagnant stream of dead matter which are constantly raised by Kal Niranjan in order to bring about influences to keep Soul caged within

213

the body.

The attempt to render into words the totality of one's thoughts at any given moment presents difficulties. There are not enough words available to make it possible. Thought, at its simplest being a rather wide band of perceptions, often confuses the chela who does not know what should be selected for his best interest. This is why one's concentration must be upon the ECK rather than anything else. Once the consciousness of the individual is put upon the ECK and filled with It there is no problem, for every word, thought, and deed is of the highest order, and he follows Its dictates naturally.

The confusion here is that man believes human beings think in words, but this is not true. Man thinks in images within a stream of consciousness. Most of the time the stream of consciousness is really what predominates in the neurotic and psychotic mind. It never has good recall, and only occasionally can it be shut off, in order to get the individual fixed in some sort of stillness within the inner self, to get him outside his psychic state of consciousness.

Those who allow this stream of consciousness to control their lives are in very poor states. Whenever a thought foists itself upon the thinker and persists in spite of his wishes, the thinker is in trouble. He must be able to call up practically any thought or memory within his whole realm of knowledge without going through his stream of consciousness.

Most religious and metaphysical systems within the earth-world lean too heavily on this stream of thought association. Out of it come the twin negative emotions, hatred and fear. This leads to the doctrine of wars and destruction, and the pursuit of power, which keeps the world in an undesirable state of turmoil.

It means then that the mission of the Mahanta on this

214

earth is to stir the millions of noninitiated into revolt against all orthodox religions. It also means that anyone who opposes the Mahanta in any of the worlds is foolish for the ECK will swiftly work in retribution. There is no wasting away of the Mahanta's strength, for it is of the power of the ECK. He does not have to prove anything, for all is there as clear as life itself. While the priest can prove any religious proposition by quoting texts from some sacred scripture, the Mahanta proves it by his very existence.

The mainspring of every civilization is its church. When that decays, the civilization decays with it. But with the ECK one finds no decay, for Its strength lies in the SUGMAD, and hence It is all powerful. Because the Living ECK Master is always with every civilization in history, those who follow the ECK find that it needs no human state of consciousness to guide it, as orthodox religions do.

No one should exploit the good and gentleness in man. But those trying to gain power in this world do so, be it in religious or other matters. To anyone who is not spiritual, spirituality always looks like hypocrisy.

Man is able to tell what comfortable lies he likes to others but he must beware of telling them to himself— not because it is immoral but because, unfortunately, he will not be able to deceive himself. One cannot live happily with a person he knows is a liar. Those in the human state of consciousness will always be ready to deceive others, while living in frustration from such states themselves. The Living ECK Master knows what is going on within each of them, but he says nothing. Every individual who lives in this attitude must himself be subjected to what he practices.

All ECK Masters who have come here to live upon this earth plane and to give spiritual assistance to those ECK chelas who desire to follow, must be above all things sincere, honest, and above reproach. But whatever they do in their human lives will have nothing to do with their spiritual lives; the two are often in opposition with one another.

By his inner powers the Living ECK Master looks at the inner state of the chela, not the outer self. If any are worthy, they will qualify to be given the higher initiations and will receive the true spiritual instruction about the royal road of ECK. At times the Mahanta will openly discourage some, because they are not inwardly receptive. He never pays heed to one's caste, color, or nationality. He is ever steady in his outlook upon all, and he sees the ECK in all, though few see It in themselves.

It is by these same inner powers that he gives chelas secret instructions at long distances, without speaking or using the written word. He will often send one of his own Mahdis in the Nuri Sarup to those who are in need of instruction and initiation. The Mahanta knows the inner states of all chelas and anticipates their actions and questions. At times his behavior may offend the general public and even some chelas, but the true seekers of the SUGMAD recognize what this means to themselves and the public.

When the initiated one is ready to cross the Bhava Sagar, the tumultuous ocean of birth, death, and rebirth, he knows the Mahanta is ready to assist him. He will not have to face the Angel of Death nor the Judge of Karma, for the Mahanta will not let him be touched by either. He is taken by the Living ECK Master to that place in the high spiritual planes which he has earned during his life on earth. Neither will he be compelled to return to this earth world in another incarnation.

The chela should never expect nor ask that the Living ECK Master fit the image which he has formed through

216

reading and listening to others about any pseudomasters. All are pseudomasters except for the Living ECK Master; he is the only authentic Master within this world. Many seekers of God make their own image of what they expect a Master to be, and, learning that the Mahanta does not fit this image, they become disappointed. They look too much for gentleness and kindness, and all the virtues which they believe should be the main qualities of a Master. They look for love when perhaps what they believe is love does not exist. Their disappointment is too deep for retreat. Sadly they turn away only to learn that what they are seeking does not exist within this world.

The Mahanta is kind, gentle, and loving to whomever he believes needs these qualities for spiritual growth; to others he might appear to be understanding, but firm and sharp in his discipline. He treats everybody according to their spiritual growth and helps each unfold individually on the path of the SUGMAD.

The ECK is the unity in the midst of diversity and multiplicity, which means that all the functions of life preexist in the SUGMAD. But IT expresses ITSELF through the ECK in the worlds of ITS own making. So it's found that the ECK is the cause of all life, for It is the medium which the SUGMAD uses to reach all existence. The universes then are the effect of the ECK. Nothing can appear in the effect which was not already in the cause. The cause is ever present in the effect because it is as much in the whole as the ECK is in the SUGMAD, and the Mahanta is in the ECK.

Separation from the Mahanta is pain, and unity with him is peace. All is within the Mahanta, for all within him is in the ECK, as well as in the SUGMAD. When this understanding rises in the Atma, there is a great burst of knowledge and unfoldment which gives It peace

217

and happiness. All conditions of space, time, and causation are within the ECK. All the universes are within It, and so is the reconciliation of all opposites. Yet It is attributeless and possesses the works of the SUGMAD, in the being and nonbeing states.

Therefore, whoever lives in the whole, and in whom the whole lives fully, is alone in his holiness. Few can share it with him, for they do not know what it is and cannot understand anyone in whom it dwells.

In finding himself, man turns his consciousess to the Mahanta, and allows the Living ECK Master to fill it. By doing so he passes through the limitations of the little self into the nonlimitations of the SUGMAD Consciousness.

It is in the little self that man craves to burst the bondage and become freed from all ills, find personal immortality and salvation. He fails for he believes that the ECK can be brought into manifestation by either written or spoken words. The truth of this is that the true word or name of the SUGMAD is Dhunatmik. IT resounds within the chela and never without, as many believe. There are the two forms of the Name. First is the Dhunatmik, which is the soundless word, and second is the Varnatmik, which is the sound of the word in many forms. The Dhunatmik exists in those regions where language is not needed. It is the smile of the lover who finds that his love exists in the heart and not on his lips nor in his deeds. One can never express in words or deeds, gestures or symbols, what the spiritual ears hear.

The Varnatmik is the great Sound of the Physical, Astral, Causal, and Mental Worlds. It is heard by the inner and outer ears, in many forms, but always as the echo of the original Sound, the Dhunatmik of the upper worlds. The chela must always take care to distinguish between the echo and original. The Dhunatmik can never be heard by the outer ears; therefore, the inner ears must be attuned to the higher vibrations of the true SUGMAD worlds.

The creative primal music of the ECK is always vibrating throughout all the universes of the SUGMAD. It is the voice of the divine Reality, the SUGMAD, vibrating into all regions like a great wave. When this primal force leaves the heart of the Ocean of Love and Mercy, It becomes the ECK, which is the Dhunatmik—the soundless, wordless Music. The Varnatmik is the Sound which breaks into many sounds, and is manifested in the lower worlds.

Those who seek God always look for the one who is able to converse with the Dhunatmik, the Inner Word: One who knows the way of the ECK. Every Soul is released through the ECK, brought out of the darkness of matter, and set free through the Mahanta, in the form of the Sound Current. As soon as the pure-consciousness is established within him, he actually hears the ECK-Current, the Dhunatmik, which is not heard by the outer ears.

At first he does not know from where the inner Sound comes, but he instinctively does know It comes from the direction which he must take. Without consciousness of the Sound, he would be in darkness. It reaches down from the Ocean of Love and Mercy pulling Souls out of the darkness of the lower worlds into the heart of the SUGMAD.

Through the ECK, the Dhunatmik, comes the creation of all the universes and all the creatures and beings, and man himself. In heaven and on earth no other name is to be given It but that of the ECK; by ECK alone can man escape the bondage of worldly ills and the Wheel of the Eighty-Four.

The divine and direct method of the ECK is natural

219

and innate in man; there are no substitutes for It. It is found within Itself. Without devotion, Soul is not purified; and without the purification of Soul there is little that man can do for himself. He must remain faithful to the Spiritual Exercises of ECK. He must set aside the gross and seek only the pure within himself, for without this there can never be any success in hearing the Sounds of the ECK, or dwelling in the heart of the SUGMAD.

The human form and mind are gross embodiments which can never have direct contact with the Dhunatmik. This ECK Dhunatmik is the cause of the consciousness in man. The essence of the ECK must be joined with man's consciousness to remove all earthly vestures that separate the two. It is through the ECK that Soul descends into the darkness of matter and mind and becomes bound. It is also through the ECK and the Mahanta, the living embodiment of the ECK, that Soul is lifted out of this darkness of matter and mind.

Unless the seeker finds the Mahanta, who is conversant with the ECK, he shall be unable to return to the true Ocean of Love and Mercy. The way of the ECK is the only escape from the caged condition of maya, the veil of illusion which keeps one in the world of matter and mind.

When the chela is no longer encumbered with the mind, he is free, happier, and finds life in the SUGMAD. Nothing can limit his activities or bar his perceptions. But he learns that knowledge of universal nature is possible only by means of a human body. All the kingdoms of the universe have their corresponding sheaths in the human system: the Physical, Astral, Causal, Mental, and Etheric. Into each sheath are woven the ECK principles, ranging from abstract factors of conscious life to relations and laws governing natural facts. Also, each plane has both the universal and individual aspects. The bodies of each individual are a microcosm in which the macrocosm dwells.

The ECK of Itself has no body. But this ECK—and not God or the SUGMAD—is in everybody, everything, and is no-thing. Therefore, the body and the embodied are not separated; they are not the same, but similar. Each Soul is given a body to wear for a divine purpose. This is the field of karma and the human world is the place of karma.

There are those who serve the Mahanta for desires and selfish purposes, and those who tirelessly strive for Truth. There are those who for fear of pain, birth, death, and other common calamities, seek sanctuary with the Mahanta to escape them. Finally there are those who, having known Reality, have established themselves in It; they alone love the Truth for truth's sake; these are the children of the ECK.

At the time of initiation the chela is imparted vital secrets, which facilitate his growth and speed up his karma. The highest, perfect directions for the Spiritual Exercises of ECK are given. These help him to unfold his inner hearing and inner sight, and with them he begins his evergrowing inward and upward pilgrimage to the SUGMAD.

At initiation the Mahanta personally, or through his Mahdis, connects the chela with the ECK Sound Current, and accompanies him all the way through the regions of Light until he reaches his home within the Ocean of Love and Mercy. All men caught in the meshes of matter cannot be released until the Mahanta connects them with the inner ECK Current. No man can tune himself in to the Sound Current, for it is only the Mahanta's own initiatory power that can do this for him.

Soul is connected with the Sound Current at initiation only by the Mahanta, whether he is there in person or not. He may have one of the Mahdis, initiate of the Fifth Plane, to do this but the initiator is only an instrument through which the initiation and connection are given.

When the connection is made, the chela develops the ability to travel by himself, in the company of the Mahanta. He is more than able to overcome the downward pull of mind and matter, and keeps ascending toward the regions of true Light. When there has been enough progress made on the path of ECKANKAR, he cannot gather any more negative karma. The earthward pull has ended and the upward pull becomes more powerful and acts upon Soul.

It is always the individual Soul, the conscious man, that is initiated and animated. Therefore, the age of the physical body will have nothing to do with the initiation, and the effectiveness and efficiency of the initiation depends on the competence and compliance of the one who receives it. The inner states of consciousness differ in different individuals. The Mahanta animates and quickens the ECK mantra, making it a mass of radiant energy; he injects his own consciousness and its subjective Light into the chela receiving the initiation, and the chela then feels the shock of spiritual consciousness. It is an unspeakable feeling of blessedness which comes upon him.

Blended in consciousness with the Mahanta, it is then that the chela rises to planes within planes. This inner elevation of consciousness results also in the expansion of consciousness. It is then that the initiated one finds an added knowledge of himself and those glories of the ECK which await him. He reaches these heights by the grace of the Living ECK Master; he would have been unable to reach them if he had not entered onto the path of ECKANKAR.

The initiate, who with great devotion is purged of his dross at the time of initiation, enters through the single eye—the straight and narrow gate—into a tremendous expansion of consciousness, which transports him with joy into a state of beingness he has never before known.

Thus begins the chela's journey to the SUGMAD; he walks on the straight and narrow path, which is as sharp as the razor's edge, and listens all the while to the ECK Sound Current. All this is accomplished while the chela is in full possession of his faculties. He finally arrives at the court of Sat Nam, ruler of the Fifth Plane, and sees this great being in Its radiant and inexpressible form. Then he realizes that the SUGMAD, the ECK, and all the rulers of the vast universes throughout the spiritual kingdom of the SUGMAD, are all one in one, and that, in reality, each is the Mahanta, the Living ECK Master. This is the greatest of all discoveries, for the Mahanta is formless in spite of having form. He is of spiritual form and material form, being many things and many forms.

The chela will come to the point where he cares nothing for cultural creeds, philosophies, civilizations, and societies. He knows they are only pale offshoots of the true Reality. The holy current of the ECK is all that counts for him while living in the physical form, but he knows that he now is of two worlds. The coming and the going of the bodies of man are of little interest to him, for he knows that this is the way of the world. But when initiated into ECKANKAR, all are free from the births and deaths of the body. All are then at rest with the SUGMAD in the Ocean of Love and Mercy.

The journey to the SUGMAD begins at the Tisra Til, the Third Eye, and from this point Soul ascends upward. Soul is cut free from all material toils and from the Kal, who has restricted It from the beginning of Its journey in this world. Proper training under the direction of the Mahanta after initiation will work wonders, and the seemingly impossible becomes possible. The finer senses become active and aware by right use, as directed by the Mahanta. At first the ECK Sound Current is weak, often imperceptible, but variable. However, by continual training, a transformation takes place and the Music of the Spheres is heard quite distinctly. Its divine and delectable Sound is of a sweetness and serenity unsurpassed by any.

This Music draws Soul upward by Its strong power, like a powerful magnet. It purifies all which Soul picked up as dross during Its sojourn on earth. As the awakened consciousness makes Soul partake of the joys of heaven It becomes a greater channel for the Mahanta to use for spreading the message of ECKANKAR. Thus Soul, severed from maya and its illusions, its seeds of desires, its hopes and fears, is liberated and established in the great Reality of ECK.

By contemplating upon the Living ECK Master, the chela discovers the fickle and faltering nature of his mind. The Mahanta removes mortality and the lower nature from Soul and gives It strength and firmness. There is only a singular sense of purpose within the God Worlds, and this brings Soul into Its own reality. It separates illusions from truth and brings to Soul the recognition of Itself as a channel for the Mahanta. Soul establishes Itself in the true light of the SUGMAD by this recognition, and few, if any, will reach these heights unless they bring themselves to that point of getting rid of the ego and accepting the Mahanta as their spiritual guide in life.

The ECK Satsang is important to the chela, for it is a part of his being in the works of ECKANKAR. Without the ECK Satsang, the true potential of the chela never becomes an actuality. Unless the grace of the SUGMAD is upon the chela, there is never born a deep aspiration for heavenly things. He cannot receive these blessings unless the ECK helps his heart to understand and hunger

224

for truth. People cannot be made to become spiritual. This is the greatest mistake made among those who desire truth, but who make no effort at finding it. They believe the Living ECK Master can give them spirituality.

This is not true, for spirituality is born in the heart of man by the grace of the Supreme Deity. When one attends an ECK Satsang, he becomes refined in the presence of others and moves in grace toward becoming an instrument of the SUGMAD. He becomes closer to the Mahanta in spirit and they can communicate secretly. The relationship between the two is of a love greater than words can express; it is the highest of any love.

The Living ECK Master has a relationship with the chela which is an ever-present inspiration. In his presence the chela finds that the dormant vitality within himself becomes a dynamic actuality which strengthens his spiritual unfoldment. The devotion of the chela for the Mahanta is divine and, therefore, their close relationship is sacred, strong, and permanent. As the chela makes his way upward, the true love between him and the Mahanta grows, and there is never any chance of its diminution.

To utter the Word, or the ECK mantra, in a special arrangement, is to build one's own future in the other worlds. This is especially true of building in the Akasha, the primal matter force. The ECK enters into the composition of all beings and things of life. It is the primary Sound of every world within the universes of the SUGMAD. The sounds of the oceans, the whistling of the winds, the rustle of trees in the forests, the beating of drums, the noises of great cities, the cries of animals, and the words and emotional sounds of people are the natural elemental sounds of the ECK.

All words are but forms of the ECK, for each is a modification of the inner Sound. This consists of the primal Sound of life and matter. The substance of the atom, its vibration, and the equality of the Sound which are inseparable in reality and in consciousness. Within the psychic worlds is the cycle of sounds. It is important that each vibration has a start, a continuation, and a finish.

Vibration is the manifestation of action by the ECK, but initiation is by the SUGMAD and carried via the Sound throughout all the universes. The chela learns this secret from the Mahanta after his Seventh initiation.

He begins to understand that the number of vibrations is the principle secret of the production of all sounds. Vibration arises in one of the Kal worlds because of the presence of substance, the reality in it. Sometimes, if the chela is on the higher spiritual planes of the SUGMAD, he will find that vibrations rise only under his origination, and not by fixed law. However, all such vibrations take place in a moment.

The ECK Sound is produced by such a vibration in the higher worlds. Because there is so much Sound, there arises the inarticulate Sound. On the lower planes the opposite is working: for each of the sounds without articulation, there must be equal sounds with articulation. In these worlds the sounds, or vibrations, must work opposite one another, the inarticulate against the articulate. This makes perfect vibrations within the matter worlds, and until these are matched there can be no music, nor words, nor sounds from man. Therefore, man must have silence and sound in equal portions, for if one overbalances the other then he will have pressures from the inner powers which will pull him one way or the other. It could even bring death to his physical body.

For example, if man spends too much time in silence, as those pseudoholy men do sitting in caves in the vastness of mighty mountains, they are not fit to serve their fellow men. They do nothing for themselves nor anything for the race of men. They become selfish in their desire for silence and receiving the powers of the ECK. When living in this state, the individual is apt to lose all he has tried to gain.

When man spends all his time with the other extreme, which is noise, he is soon driven crazy. He cannot live in this state for long without losing all that he has desired of the SUGMAD. Therefore, unless he balances the periods of time for receiving and giving out vibrations, there will be an imbalance in him which will bring a loss of spiritual growth.

The right act is the act which best serves the progress of all. It shall bring the greatest good to the greatest number of people. It shall put all beings of all worlds in accord with the will of the SUGMAD.

The chela never consciously makes such efforts to do the right thing for all, for if he did, much of his time would be spent in trying to decide what would be the most universally just thing to do. He gives himself up to the Mahanta and allows the Living ECK Master to work through him. Whatever he does is always in the name of the Mahanta, and therefore, most of his actions will be right. But opposition to right action will always be strong, so he must consider that there will be good and evil times, and proper and improper seasons for doing right actions. He should not have to put his mind to making such decisions, but rather let the ECK use him for right deeds, as It knows best.

True judgment takes into consideration the necessity of the circumstances, the requirements of the particular spiritual evolution, and the time period and world system in which the particular Soul in question dwells. But there is a main aspect to this, and that is love for all life. Right speech, right duty, and right hearing are of the same pattern. By depending upon the guidance of the Mahanta, by becoming a divine channel, one falls into the patterns of right acts, right speech, right duty, and right hearing. By all this, he finds true spiritual growth and eventually works out all his karma in one lifetime. He enters into the heavenly worlds at last, never having to return to this plane in any incarnation.

During this life on earth, one finds conflicts with his domestic duties to his household, state, and country. He is often called to duty for defense of the homeland, or to take part in some political act, for some act of good for humanity, or for a religious or moral purpose. Sometimes the call of Soul will cause the individual to cast aside everything to follow it. The call of the Mahanta is the highest of all, for it is the spiritual beckoning of the SUGMAD to come home again. This call is imperative and cannot be weighed against any other condition.

If he is willing to give up everything in his life to follow the call of the Mahanta, then let him do so. It means that he will have peace of heart, but will suffer in body and spirit from the taunts and insults of life around him. He must be forever dedicated to the Mahanta, for being so then will the grace of all life be given to him, whether he is in rags or wears rich garments upon his back.

He shall receive little praise for what he gives in life to the divine Reality, nor shall anyone appreciate his sacrifices. He will be reduced in social and human stature, but his spiritual self will be like a shining giant among pygmies. He will be in love with all people, all creatures, and all life. But he will be reviled, spat upon, and hated for the spiritual light he carries with him.

He will find the Mahanta's name torn to shreds, his life always in danger, and his reputation continually shattered. The masses will not like truth being thrust upon them, and they will be used by the Kal to destroy whatever body, or vessel, the Mahanta wears at the time he is in the world as the Living ECK Master.

It is only then that the chela realizes that life here on earth as the spiritual channel for the Mahanta is not without its dangers and problems. He truly learns then who the Mahanta really is; he learns what spiritual greatness has been thrust upon the Mahanta. He learns that he himself is to become a co-worker in the field of the divine Reality.

He will also learn that, although the Mahanta is with him every moment, day and night, he is truly in a lonely position. No one knows or understands the spiritual cloak he wears, except a handful of those who follow the ECK. But he will know that always he is in the protecting love and light of the Mahanta, the Living ECK Master, and no harm can ever touch him.

Thus ends the first book of the Shariyat-Ki-Sugmad.

Index

232

233

235

Earth *(continued)*
Shariyat on, *xii*
SUGMAD manifested on, 28, 109
thought stream of, 144
world, 92, 97
ECK. *See also* Sound Current
adversaries of, 130
and chela, 13, 47, 84, 131, 213
all-embracing, 95, 141, 184
as God-knowledge, *xiii*
children of the, 6, 119, 221
creation by, 23, 24, 43, 50, 51, 55, 56, 217
creative principle, 25, 163
currents, 25, 208
eternal, 27, 115
expression of God, 3, 24, 203
flows, 78
holy works of, 79, 127, 163
initiation into, 7
in Spiritual Hierarchy, 87
Kingdom of the, 106
Lifestream, 17
love and, 2, 126, 128
Mahanta and, 38, 76, 147, 176
manifested in, 11, 24
mystery of, 193
path of, *xii*, 6, 9, 30, 32, 33, 74, 77, 93, 97, 98, 123, 126, 133, 148, 150, 155, 156, 164, 175, 176, 180, 181, 182, 191, 196, 207, 222
power of, 24, 162, 171, 176, 177, 179, 198, 209
principles of, 34, 158
purpose of, 128, 198
qualities of the, 1, 6, 208, 217
realization of, 17, 143, 152
sound of, 2, 24, 25, 86, 105, 126, 138, 224
sovereign state, 35
Spirit, 93, 99, 100, 159
Spiritual Exercises of, 138,

139, 144, 154, 161
teachings of, 11, 170, 173
universal, 123, 195, 217
versus Kal, 125
works of, 80, 119, 127, 141, 144, 158, 163, 172, 185, 202
wrath of, 5, 183
ECK Adept(s). *See* ECK Master(s)
ECK Master(s), *xii*, 77, 87, 90, 95, 96, 101, 113, 126, 129, 131, 160, 172. *See also* Castrog; Fubbi Quantz; Geutan; Gopal Das; Jalal-ud-din'l-Rumi; Kabir; Kai-Kuas; Lai Tsi; Living ECK Master; Mahanta; Malati; Peddar Zaskq; Rama; Rami Nuri; Rebazar Tarzs; Regnard; Sepher, Shamus-i-Tabriz; Yaubl Sacabi
explained ECK, 79, 200
faith in, 83
first, 54
home of, 78
initiation, 2, 3
love of, 134
Soul joins with, 75
surrender to, 8
reach fifth stage of development, 74
ECK Marg. *See* ECK: path of
ECKANKAR
Ancient Science of Soul Travel, 12
aspect of SUGMAD in, 29
equilibrium, 136
follower of, 75, 157
path of, *xii*, 32, 34, 64, 74, 97, 106, 146, 158, 161
philosophy of, 118, 142
preaching, 60
principles of, *xiii*, 155
true Master of, 96

236

true teachings of, 79, 94, 96
works of, 18, 66, 99, 100, 119,
   158, 179, 185
ECKist
   ECK makes the, 208
   enters into Atma Lok, 206
   experiences of, 190, 196
   goes beyond phenomena, 189
   not a mystic, 203
   practice dying daily, 99
   practice Kundun, 77, 83, 177
   recognizes no other religion,
      98
   special person, 201
ECKshar, 7, 152. *See also* Self-
   Realization
ECK-Vidya, 70, 71
Ede, 54
Eden, Garden of, 54
Ego, 19, 24, 32, 84, 101, 125,
   158, 198–99. *See also*
   Human consciousness; Self:
   little
Egyptians, 35
Elam, 46
Elementals, 88
Empire of the Sun. *See* Mu
Energy, 38, 48, 87, 88, 222
Enlightened, enlightenment
   desires of Soul, 4
   knowledge, 105
   Self-Realization, 71
   Souls, *xiv*
   spiritually, 3, 30, 104, 114,
      142, 160
Envy, 47
Epochs. *See* Age; Yuga
Eshwar-Khanewale, 92
Essence. *See also* ECK
   of God, 12, 29, 42, 90
   of life, 1, 186
Etheric
   body, 70, 220
   mind, 70, 78

Plane, 23, 75, 89, 91, 177
Eternity
   beyond time, 11
   freedom of, *xiv*
   Gods of, 79
   of Ocean of Love and Mercy,
      41
   life in, 45, 108, 114, 155, 168,
      209
   Soul and, 64, 69, 115, 116,
      117, 149
   truth of, 144
Europe, 54, 60
Everlasting Gospel, 200. *See also*
   ECK
Evil, 78, 101, 126, 133

Faith
   belief, 64, 72, 98, 190, 192,
      195, 207
   in ECK, 80, 84, 110, 177
   in Kal, 104
   Living ECK Master and, 14,
      106, 120, 213
   revival of, 170
   riddle of, 164
   spiritual knowing as, 39
   unwavering, 96
Faqiti Monastery, 92
Fasting, 4
Fear, 47, 80, 125, 150, 198, 214
Fifth
   Circle. *See* Initiate: Fifth Circle
   Plane. *See* Soul Plane
   root race. *See* Aryan race
First
   Cause, 7
   root race. *See* Polarian race
Fivefold bodies of the Mahanta,
   112
Five passions of the mind. *See*
   Mind: passions of the, five

237

Fourth
  Circle. *See* Initiate: Fourth
    Circle
  Plane. *See* Mental Plane
  root race. *See* Atlantean race
Freedom
  emotional, 131
  from pain, 136
  Jivan Mukti. *See* Jivan Mukti
  liberation of Soul. *See*
    Liberation: of Soul
  of eternity, *xiv*
  of Living ECK Master, 123,
    129, 160
  Mahanta never interferes in,
    110, 113, 130
  man desires, 178
  must be rewon, 28
  requirement for meeting the
    Mahanta, 126
  spiritual, 63, 120, 194
  state of, 4
  struggle for, 22, 39, 220
Fubbi Quantz, 12, 92
Future, 70, 109, 114, 115, 121

Gare-Hira Temple of Golden
  Wisdom, 92
Gates of Heaven. *See* Heaven:
  gates of
Geutan, 58
Gobi Desert, 60, 92
God. *See also* SUGMAD
  attributes of, 145
  chosen one(s) of, 93, 112
  consciousness, 218. *See also*
    God-Realization
  Co-worker with. *See* Co-
    worker: with SUGMAD
  death of man's, 39
  gift from, 115, 169
  -governed, 83
  grace of, 4, 14, 32, 74, 80,

152, 224, 225
  -knowledge, *xiii*, 67, 114
  knowledge of, 55
  issues of, 18
  line between Kal and, 94
  love of, 128, 130
  manifestation of, 49, 103, 109,
    110
  names of, 41, 84
  path to, *xiii*, 12, 30, 75, 106,
    136, 161
  principle of, 142
  realization of, 142, 206. *See*
    also God-Realization
  seeker of, 13, 89, 108
  universe of, 219
  Voice of, 6, 152. *See also* ECK;
    Sound Current
  will of, 34, 110, 142
  worlds of, 93, 103, 224
God Consciousness. *See* God-
  Realization
God-eaters. *See* Eshwar-
  Khanewale
Godhead, 11, 29, 75, 188, 205
Godman. *See also* Living ECK
    Master; Mahanta
  eternal, 40
  face of, 13
  living, 17, 19, 21
  Living ECK Master, 12, 92,
    195
  love of, 10
  message of, 10
  uses scriptures, 11
  will of, 19
God-Realization, 14, 29, 31, 37,
    38, 67, 76, 80, 101, 108, 117,
    118, 126, 142, 146, 155, 218
Gods of Eternity, nine
  unknown. *See* Eternity:
    gods of
God-Vidya. *See* God: -knowl-
    edge

238

240

Lemurian race, 56
Liberation, 131, 136
  attitude and, 135
  death before, 132
  of Soul, 18, 25, 38, 40, 63, 74,
    98, 115, 130, 131, 135, 153,
    181, 194, 219
  spiritual, 7, 71
Life
  and ECK, 68, 177, 186
  and embodiments, 111
  and love, 107, 156
  and Mahanta, 93, 113, 119
  cell of, 50
  chela's, 23, 83, 157
  endures, 101
  everlasting, 28
  good of, 116
  hardships of, 108, 114
  heaven after, 106
  illusions of, 133, 147, 159
  lifetimes, 7, 37, 72, 75, 92,
    208, 228
  seeks to keep, 149
  source of all, 113, 114, 205
  stress of, 144
  SUGMAD and, 84, 104
  way of, 110
Light
  all shall have, 3
  and Love, 129
  and Sound, 42, 68, 71, 107,
    126, 133, 143, 145, 151, 162,
    185
  becomes stronger, 96
  bring to all peoples, 93
  Divine, xiv, 162
  holy, 8, 115
  lives in, 179
  of Mahanta, 5, 222
  of SUGMAD, 224
  of the ECK, 141
  of worlds, 113
  seeks before ready, 119, 151

  shadow instead of, 98
  Shariyat as true, xiv
  symbol of individuality, 24
  true, 144
  worlds of, 74
Light body. See Astral body:
    Light body
Lightning Worlds, 76
Lila, 14
Living ECK Master. See also
    Mahanta
  acts of, 127
  and civilization, 111, 215
  and ECK, 141, 145, 162
  and grace, 14, 80, 222
  as Mahanta, 95, 118, 126, 228
  authentic Master, 217
  blessings from, 85, 212
  chela and, 1, 66, 73, 74, 108,
    111, 123, 131, 172, 180, 192,
    197, 225, 227
  chosen one learns that he is,
    112
  criticize, 80, 98
  defends God-power, 119
  Dhyana, 138, 139. See also
    Living ECK Master:
    presence of; Mahanta:
    presence of
  gifts of God via, 106, 121, 149
  initiates Soul, 7, 9, 64
  in Spiritual Hierarchy, 87
  karma and, 78, 134, 140, 143,
    145
  liberation. See also Liberation:
    of Soul
  Light and Sound through,
    107, 152
  love for, 124
  manifestation of God, 109,
    115
  meet with, 17, 65, 97, 126,
    132, 137. See also Darshan
  mission of, 13, 29, 47, 161

distributor of the works of
  ECK, 131
eternal, 33, 35
food of ECK from, 147
gift from, 106, 119, 150
Godman, 21, 92, 195
grace of, 154
guides chela, 65, 73, 75, 116,
  130, 148, 155
Guru, 74, 103
historical, 33
Inner Master, 76, 77, 152, 156
in Spiritual Hierarchy, 87, 90,
  191
is of ECK, 76, 154–55
Living ECK Master as, 118,
  129, 227, 228
Mahantaship, 95
personification of Truth, 142
powers of, 216
presence of, 14, 77, 138
strength of, 215
SUGMAD and, 27, 29, 37, 44,
  79, 86, 105, 108, 136, 154,
  177, 182
teaches chela, 34, 94, 96, 116,
  127, 128, 140, 145, 186
travel with, 169
two sides of the, 39–40
will of, 130
Mahanta Consciousness. *See*
  Mahanta: consciousness
Maha Kal. *See* Kal Niranjan
Maha Kal Lok, 89
Maharaj, 191
Mahavakyis, 191. *See also* Silent
  One(s)
Mahaya Guru, the, 91
Mahdis, 162, 171, 175, 176, 177,
  180, 181, 186, 197, 216, 222.
  See also Initiate: Fifth Circle
Malati, 55
Man, 88
Manas (part of mind) 8, 200

Manas. *See* Mental body;
  Mental Plane
Manifestation, 19, 46, 72, 88,
  90, 95, 103, 110, 113, 152
Mantra, 138, 162, 171, 173, 222,
  225
Manvantara, 16
Marg, 7
Master. *See also* ECK Master(s);
  Living ECK Master;
  Mahanta
false, 5, 99, 125.
Matter
  beyond, 26
  dead, 213
  downward pull of, 222
  physical, 135
  plane of, 97
  space and time, 28, 30, 48, 65,
    87, 88
  world of, 69, 92, 101, 220
Maya, 15, 141, 159, 220, 224. *See*
  also Illusion
Meditation, 167
Medium, 128
Melnibora, 55
Mental body, 70, 129, 220
Mental Plane
  bond, 78
  Brahm Lok, 75, 206
  ECK distributed to, 177
  high, 206
  intellectual, 166
  Kal will attack from, 143
  of lower worlds, 23
  Mahdis above, 197
  Master works on, 10
  mystic does not go above, 203
  mystical consciousness, 205
  Par Brahm, 89, 91
  phenomenon of, 110, 189
  Pindi, 77
  realms of 18, 200
  Truth is beyond, 200

Mental Plane *(continued)*
    Varnatmik is heard in, 218
    Voice of, 6
Mental Sharir. *See* Mental body
Mer Kailash, 91
Mercy, 37, 78, 107, 182
Metaphysical, 98, 193, 214
Microcosm, 221
Mind
    and Truth, 110, 200
    Buddhi, 200
    channel for negative, 37
    Chitta, 200
    creates and controls body,
        159
    doctors of, 106
    downward pull of, 222
    fickle nature of, 224
    impure, 144
    infects all, 36
    limited, 84
    link between heaven and
        earth, 22
    Mahanta as king of, 38
    memory and, 75
    of man, 117, 209
    passions of the, five, 85, 100,
        131, 165. *See also* Anger;
        Attachment; Greed; Lust;
        Vanity
    power of, 46
    products of, 160
    proper use of, 169
    transformation of, 142
    used to live within physical
        plane, 69
    world of, 111, 220
Mind body. *See* Mental body
Mind-realization, 117
Miracle(s), 79, 93, 99, 105, 109,
    118, 121, 149
Mission
    of chela, 66, 69
    of Mahanta, 105, 214

    of Soul, 42, 65, 68, 74, 173
Missionary, 130, 164
Moha. *See* Attachment
Moksha Temple of Golden
    Wisdom, 13, 92
Mongoloid race, 60
Moon Worlds, 76, 137
Motion, 65
Mountain world. *See* Surati Lok
Mu, 58, 59, 60
Music
    heavenly white, 2, 86
    of ECK, 126, 138, 139, 219
    of flute, 67
    of heaven, 2, 6, 7, 86, 121
    of the SUGMAD, 2, 25, 81
    of the Spheres, 24, 224
    of woodwinds, 68
Muslims, 35
Mystery schools, *xiii*, 195
Mystic, 162, 202, 203, 205
Myths, 193

Naacal, *xi*, 12
Nada. *See* Sound Current: other
    names for
Nada Bindu. *See* Sound
    Current: other names for
Namayatan Temple of Golden
    Wisdom, 91
Name, 85, 218
Nameless plane. *See* Anami Lok
Nameless Void, 85
Narrow way, 140
Nature, forces of, 178
Negative agent, 37
Negative force. *See* Kal Niranjan
Negative pole, 87
Negative worlds. *See* Worlds,
    lower
Nether world, 88, 148
Ninth circle. *See* Initiate: Ninth
    Circle

246

Nine unknown Gods of
Eternity. *See* Eternity: gods
of
Nine worlds, 148
Niranjan. *See* Kal Niranjan
Nirguna, 14
Nirvana, 34, 188
Nirvikalpa, 139, 142, 205
Non-ECKist, 185
Noumenon, 30
No Thing, 36
No-thing, worlds of, 86
Nuri Sarup. *See* Astral body

Obedient, 64, 120
to Living ECK Master, 148
to Word of SUGMAD, 3
Ocean of Love and Mercy
at rest in, 223
body of SUGMAD, 120
ECK flows down from, 38,
49, 88, 110, 219
eternity of, 41
home of Supreme Being, 6,
68, 85, 86, 91
includes all qualities of
SUGMAD, 2
Mahanta rules over all planes
from, 90
Mahanta with Soul in, 105
name of SUGMAD, 188
return to, 220
primordial Mahanta, 33
Soul enters into, 96, 101, 207
transported to, 9
true spiritual home, 159–60
Occultism, 98, 193
Omkar, 46
Omnipotence, 1, 3, 41
Omnipresence, 1, 94, 112, 129
Omniscience, 1, 41
Opposite(s), 14, 27, 87, 94, 226
Order of Vairagi Masters, 9, 22,

90, 172, 191
Orthodox, 119, 166
Osiris, 35
Outer Master, 212
Out-of-consciousness
projection, *xiii*

Pacific Ocean, 60
Padma Samba, the, 91
Pain, 78, 80, 101, 120, 136, 151,
194, 212, 217
Pantheism, 204
Par Brahm, 89
Par Brahm Lok, 91
Paradise, 148
Paradox, 94, 203, 210
Paramatma, 188
Param Akshar Temple of
Golden Wisdom, 91
Passion, human, 94
Passions of the mind. *See* Mind:
passions of the, five
Past, 70, 109, 110, 114, 121
Past life (lives), 74, 78, 99, 126,
132, 187
Path of ECK. *See* ECK: Path of
Peace
for mankind, 34
government decrees, 201
of heart, 28
of mind, 212
in heavenly worlds, 147
in human experience, 100
in physical world, 73, 136,
159
in universe, 41
religions and, 108
Satsangs and, 185
Shanti, 67
through love, 133
through unity with Mahanta,
217
Perception, 117, 214

247

248

Rod of ECK Power, 90, 160, 191
Romans, 35
Root race, 55, 56, 59, 60. *See also*
Aryan race; Atlantean race;
Hyperborean race; Lemur-
ian race; Mongoloid race;
Polarian race; Zohar race
Rules, 111
Rulers of planes. *See* Agam
Purusha; Alakh Purusha;
Alaya Purusha; Anami
Purusha; Brahm; Elam;
Hukikat Purusha; Jot
Niranjan; Kal Niranjan;
Omkar; Par Brahm;
Ramchar; Saguna Brahm;
Sat Nam; Sat Purusha;
Sohang

Sach Khand, 2, 67, 86, 89. *See
also* Soul Plane
Saguna, 14
Saguna Brahm, 89, 206
Saguna Lok, 75, 89, 91. *See also*
Etheric: Plane
"Sa-ham," 15
Sahasra-dal-Kanwal, 76, 92
Saint(s), 7, 9, 103
Sakapori Temple of Golden
Wisdom, 92
Samadhi, 139, 205. *See also*
Nirvikalpa
Sanskrit writings, *xi*
Sat Guru, 65, 74
Sat Kanwal-Anda Lok, 75. *See
also* Astral Plane
Sat Lok, 75. *See also* Soul Plane
Sat Nam, 89, 223
all life returns to, 3
life fashioned after, 44
ruler, 2, 45, 46
statements uttered to, by
SUGMAD, *xiv*

SUGMAD manifests as, 2, 78
world of, 23, 67
Sat Purusha, *xiv*, 89
Sata Visic Palace, 91
Satsang, 164, 176, 177, 180, 185,
224, 225
Saturn, 45
Satya Yuga. *See* Yuga: Satya
Savior, 99, 104, 112, 181
Scripture
of ECKANKAR, *xi*, 172
religious, 79
Second Circle, initiate of the.
See Initiate: Second Circle
Second root race. *See*
Hyperborean race
Secret kingdom, 4
Secret teachings, 76
Security, 31, 152
Seed sound, 6
Seeing, 22. *See also* Being;
Knowing
Seeker
extroverted, 202
introverted, 204
of a savior, 181
of gifts from Mahanta, 149
of God, 150, 209, 217, 219
preferences of, 151
transformation of, 171
true, 216
Seership. *See* Prophets
Self, 8, 17, 209
inner, 100
little, 142, 169, 218
radiant, 85
real, 26
Self-discipline, 18, 173
Self-Realization
divine birth as, 27
consciousness of, 7, 198–99
experience of, 173
know self, 209
on Fifth Plane, 155

252

253

256

creation of, 88
destruction of, 180
life within, 93
lower and higher, 71
of God, 19, 42, 113, 137, 149, 170, 185
of SUGMAD, 95, 103, 218
of the ECK, 65
physical, 148, 183
planes of, 69, 79, 90
riddle of, 163
running of, 74
solid, 151
spirit of, 111–12
unity of, 199
Untold region, 78. *See also* Anami Lok
Upanishads, the, *xi*
Utopia, 182

Vadan, primal, 1. *See also* Sound Current: other names for
Vairag. *See* Detachment
Vairagi Masters, 22, 31, 205. *See also* ECK Master(s); Order of Vairagi Masters
Vanity, 85, 100, 166, 172
Varkas, 55, 56
Varnatmik, 1, 2, 218, 219
Varuna, 35
Vedas, *xi*
Vehicle, 38, 64, 73, 110, 113
Venus, 13, 45, 92
Vibration(s), 149, 163, 226, 227
Viewpoint, 18
Vi-Guru, 7, 9, 80, 106, 112. *See also* Living ECK Master; Mahanta
Virgin, 111
Vishnu, 15, 35
Vision, 8, 39, 115, 137, 162, 188, 200

Voice. *See also* ECK; Sound Current
of the SUGMAD, 1, 2, 3, 5, 6, 8, 42, 68, 103, 105, 113, 151
Void, 34, 36, 42, 85, 156
Volapuk. *See* Silent One(s)

Warriors of SUGMAD, 4
Water, 111
Water test, 9
"Way of the Eternal," *xi*
Way of submission, 8
Wheel
of Awagawan, 46. *See also* Wheel: of Eighty-Four, the
of Becoming, 17. *See also* Wheel: of Eighty-Four, the
of Life. *See* Wheel: of Eighty-Four, the
of Eighty-Four, the, 17, 66, 131, 143, 147, 154, 190, 219
Will
divine, 64
of Mahanta, 19, 97, 130
of SUGMAD, 18, 87, 107, 110, 120
proper use of, 169
willpower, 138
Wind, 67
Wisdom
as deep realization, 173
divine, 79, 169
Divine Flame, 79
esoteric, 41
gained by changes, 128
knowledge alone is not, 193
love and, 129
source of, 121
understanding of, 4
whole of, 76
wise one, 147
Word of God. *See also* ECK
already done, 116

257